Energy Medicine
for Animals

Energy Medicine for Animals

THE BIOENERGETICS OF ANIMAL HEALING

DIANE BUDD

FINDHORN PRESS

Findhorn Press
One Park Street
Rochester, Vermont 05767
www.findhornpress.com

Findhorn Press is a division of Inner Traditions International

Disclaimer
The information in this book is given in good faith and is neither intended to diagnose
any physical or mental condition nor to serve as a substitute for informed medical advice
or care. The author of this book does not dispense medical advice nor prescribe the use of
any food or technique as a form of treatment for medical problems. Please contact your
health professional for medical advice and treatment. Neither author nor publisher can
be held liable by any person for any loss or damage whatsoever which may arise directly or
indirectly from the use of this book or any of the information therein.

Cataloging-in-Publication Data for this title is available from the Library of Congress

ISBN 978-1-62055-840-9 (print)
ISBN 978-1-62055-841-6 (ebook)

Printed and bound in the United States by Versa Press Inc.

10 9 8 7 6 5 4 3 2 1

Contributor: Melana Gerber
Illustrations by Diane Budd
Edited by Alexandra Lawrence and Nicky Leach
Text design, layout and illustrations by Damian Keenan
This book was typeset in Adobe Garamond Pro and Museo Sans with
Calluna Sans used as a display typeface.

To send correspondence to the author of this book, mail a first-class letter to the
author c/o Inner Traditions • Bear & Company, One Park Street, Rochester, VT 05767,
USA, and we will forward the communication, or contact the author directly at
www.healinganimals.co.za

This book is dedicated to all creatures,
big and small, who share our world with us.
They make this world a better place.

Contents

Preface

Diane's Story

I believe that each of us is unique, and that our interests in life are often reflected in our work. I'm extremely fortunate in that my way of life has become my work. I have always been both interested in the more spiritual side of life and also a skeptic, and ironically, it was my skepticism that led me to my current occupation. In fact, I initially set out to prove that animal communication was impossible.

Yet I was fascinated. If it were possible, then could I talk to my own animals? How amazing would that be? Having been an animal lover all my life, talking to my animals was one of the top ten things I could possibly wish for. Luckily for me, my wish was granted, and it has led me on one of the most incredible journeys I could ever have undertaken.

For many years after I first learned how to communicate with animals, I followed certain visualization techniques to get me into a relaxed state. Then I would begin the process of connecting, literally going through it step by step in my mind until I felt a heart connection. Sometimes I would simply know that I had connected, and at other times my heart would actually physically ache and I would get teary at the overwhelming sense of love I experienced.

Over time things got much easier and I began to follow the path of least resistance, which lay in not overthinking anything. Then one day I realized I had come a full 180 degrees and could not remember the last time I had done the "steps." By then, things pretty much happened naturally.

The next step of my journey took me backwards in time to my early twenties, when I discovered gardening. I began with the usual flower gardening, progressing to vegetables and then to herbs. Only years later did I realize that this was my soul time and a brilliant outlet from stress. I inherited my green fingers from my grandmother and my mom, who also loves gardening. It's something I will always be thankful for, as it's brought me so much pleasure. I am at my happiest when I'm barefoot and surrounded by plants and my animals.

Moving forward again, after practicing animal communication for a while, I felt I needed to do more. I struggled for years to find something that complemented animal communication, experimenting with different treatments, such as Bach flower remedies and tissue salts. They did work, but they didn't give me the powerful results I was looking for.

One day I had just finished teaching a workshop in Johannesburg and was browsing a bookstore at the airport, looking for something to read on the plane. I bought a book by Elizabeth Whiter called *The Animal Healer*. In it she spoke of her journey of discovery and zoopharmacognosy. It was what I had been unconsciously searching for. Zoopharmacognosy facilitates the process that allows animals to self-select their own remedies. It gave me the results I had been searching for, and more, taking me full circle to playing with plants again.

I went on to study Applied Zoopharmacognosy with Caroline Ingraham in England. As time went by, I started to move past my self-imposed rule of doing readings by distance only, and I began to do readings in person. I would arrive to do a zoopharmacognosy session with an animal and then either the owner or the animal would start asking questions or deliver a message.

It got to the point where I couldn't do an animal communication session without taking my plant extracts along, too, and vice versa. The two modalities complemented each other, and even more importantly, the animals really loved it and responded even better when I did both. The truth is, we all want to be heard and we all need healing in some form.

Remembering back to my initial visualizations when attempting to connect with an animal, I began to wonder what happens on an energetic level in both the human's and the animal's energy field. Was what I was visualizing in my mind's eye actually happening, or was something totally different taking place?

The illustrations in Barbara Ann Brennan's books, *Hands of Light* and *Light Emerging*, fascinated me. I have always enjoyed giving healing, and her illustrations seemed to prove that there was indeed something going on in certain levels of the body. And the more I wondered about it, the more I felt an overwhelming need to somehow find out what that was and then to document it.

Life sometimes gets in the way, though, and the idea was put aside for a while. Then one day, after I had spent several frustrating hours on the internet (yet again) doing research to try and understand what I had just seen in a session, I began to realize that there really was no information on the subject out there.

It was then that Melana came to mind. We had known each other for several years, attended some workshops together, and found that on psychic levels we picked up a lot of the same type of information, albeit in slightly different ways. Although I can see auras and read energetic information in my mind's eye when doing a session, Melana can actually see energy fields, something I find fascinating and aspire to. So I wondered if she might be able to see what was going on.

An email later, and it turned out that Melana was just as curious as I was and willing to give it a go. Although I honestly had no expectations, I was in a place of nonattachment and wanted to satisfy my curiosity. So we set up a process whereby I went through my normal routine during a healing session, and she watched what happened energetically and noted it down. Often I would pick something up and be thinking about how to solve it and she had picked up the same thing. It was great being able to get the same information and have it validated by a colleague. The information we uncovered was nothing like we had expected, and it took us completely by surprise. The rest is history and makes up the content of this book.

Melana's Story

As a small child, I often experienced the very real presence of Spirit in one form or another. Back then, I thought this was something that everyone "saw" or "knew." I didn't know that what I was seeing and feeling was auras and the movement of energy in the body. To me, it was always simply extra information about who someone was and how they functioned. Only much later did I learn that this ability is a "gift."

During my teens this gift went dormant, and it was only in my twenties that my insatiable desire to understand the way the universe worked led me to rediscover it. I began to learn about auras and energy, but only truly experienced working with energy for the first time at a group healing event. I can recall feeling the flow of energy as I placed my hands on someone, with no intention other than to send them love. Instead, I became aware of what they were feeling, both physically and emotionally. I started seeing not only lights, shadows, and glimmers around people but also those who had passed into Spirit. Although it was a frightening experience, it started my journey into the psychic and spiritual realms.

I realized I needed a way to control this flow of information, so I attended a psychic development workshop. There I learned how to communicate and co-operate with my guides, interpret the information I was receiving, and close down the ability at will. As you can imagine, this led to a lot of experimenting with my ability.

When Diane approached me to work with her and observe the processes that take place when there is intentional communication between an animal and a healer, I was immediately intrigued. I was also interested to learn more about another psychic's methods of communication, and to compare it to my own understanding. Diane and I had worked on psychic exercises together in the past and received very similar information, so I thought there would be a natural synergy between us. This hunch was correct. I also found that eavesdropping on her conversations with the animals enhanced my own ability to hear and see, and explained a lot of what I found perplexing about this form of communication.

I was astounded by the detail of the information that we received, and to witness the way the remedies interacted with the animals was truly revealing and beautiful. I was also surprised by the insight these "domesticated" animals have into us as humans, and by their sometimes humorous and always accurate observations of our behavior and needs.

Doing this work truly is a privilege, and it has given me even greater respect for the "animal people" who share our planet and whom I have always loved.

Introduction

If you're reading this book, there's a good chance you've heard of animal communication. You may have even asked an animal communicator to work with your animal, and it's changed how you think and the way you interact with animals. For humans, connecting with an animal is somewhat out of the ordinary. It is definitely not instinctive or a survival tool that we need. As so few people do it consciously, it is considered strange by some. To those who have been practicing it for years, though, it seems perfectly normal. Is it not natural to listen when someone speaks to us? Why then is it so hard for us to listen to animals? Could it be that we see them as a lower species or of a lower mind?

The moment you accept the possibility of animal communication, and that everything is composed of energy, you cannot be the same person you were before. A shift occurs, and your vibratory level changes. Your interaction with animals changes, sometimes without your even being aware of it, and you also become more intuitive and empathic toward the whole of humanity. That is what animals teach us.

So why would you read a book like this? Mainly to understand your animal and what happens to both of you energetically as you interact with each other. Often we are aware that something is not right with our animals, but we're not sure exactly what. Gaining another level of understanding can bring in healing, whether you are doing it consciously or not.

In our research we worked with many different animals and found that the information differs between species. For example, when a dog hears another dog barking and stands dead still, their energy field looks like a satellite dish. Horses operate more on scent, and the satellite effect isn't as pronounced with them. Cats are very much about will and power, and they tend to respond differently on an emotional level from horses and dogs. For this book, we focus mainly on horses, dogs, and cats, documenting the changes in their auric field during a session with an animal communicator and/or healer.

1

Auras

Most people are aware of energy in some way, and it affects our behavior, even though we might not be able to see it or understand the process in a scientific way. It may be that you walk into a room one day and feel joy and happiness, and at other times, it makes you feel uncomfortable, or you simply know that something isn't right.

You may even have looked at a horizon covered in trees and seen a faint haze above them. This is the energy field of the trees. For most people, though, it takes years of working on expanding consciousness to begin to gain a true understanding of energy fields. Although only very few people are able to see this complex energy system clairvoyantly or with the naked eye, over the centuries, adepts from various religions have spoken about seeing light around people's heads or bodies. In fact, energy fields have been studied and documented by yogis and psychics in the East for over five thousand years. Despite this, it has taken the Western world a long time to accept and embrace their existence.

Atoms are often described as nature's building blocks, and to an extent this is true. Our bodies and everything around us, from tables and chairs to plants and planets, are made up of atoms, molecules, and cells. Due to the density of the human body, most people cannot see with the naked eye how all these particles combine to make up the body, or anything else for that matter. Together, however, these create and are also influenced by the electrical and magnetic energy field around us.

In recent years, quantum physicists have developed the equipment necessary to gather scientific evidence to prove the existence of the human energy field. For example, instruments have been developed to measure the electrical currents and frequencies that emanate from the heart (you may have heard of the ECG machine). We are now able to see a reflection of our life force and health through scientific instruments and computers. As a result, modern science has finally acknowledged that we are composed of energy.

In essence, an aura is an electromagnetic form of consciousness that transmits and receives multidimensional aspects of you, as well as of every other thing on the planet. When we "see" auras, whether with the naked eye or via our sixth sense, we see another aspect of people and animals, and it helps us to understand ourselves and others better.

Anything that grows or has life will have variations in its aura. Because the distribution of light particles and wavelengths in an electromagnetic field varies greatly, auras are often perceived by the human eye and brain as a blend of colors. They're not just about colors, though; they're also about shapes, textures, sizes, patterns, and hues.

This energy tells the story of who and what you are for those who know how to read it, and it also tells an energy practitioner where to focus healing. It serves as a guide for an animal healing practitioner, too, reflecting physical concerns, both past and present. The information that we can retrieve from an energy field also opens up healing on emotional and mental levels.

From the perspective of the animal healing practitioner, every aspect of that animal's life is documented in their aura, like a blueprint of their life. While it's not always possible to pick up each and every moment in their lives, some things make a bigger imprint in the energy field than others. It's a bit like when you walk on the beach and leave your footprints in the sand. If you walk near the water, your footsteps will appear much deeper and heavier. If you walk slightly away from the water, your footsteps will appear much lighter, and it's also easier to walk. When the tide comes in, it washes some of the imprints away while others remain. Energy fields work the same way; sometimes life is hard and leaves its imprint, while at other times things run smoothly and the imprints or memories are not as deep or noticeable.

Horse Energy Fields or Aura

In metaphysical theory, all animals are evolved to different levels, as they are here on this planet for soul evolvement, just as we are. They eat, breathe, and live just like we do. They feel all of the varying degrees of emotions that we experience as humans, from anger and grief to depression and even tears of laughter, or tears of sorrow or joy. They also feel physical pain to the same intensity as humans.

Much like a human, a horse's aura is comprised of a multilayered energy field that surrounds its body. The physical body is innermost, followed by the emotional, mental, and spiritual bodies. Each layer extends beyond the last one and reflects that aspect of the horse. Because they are a different species to us, though, there are slight variations in their field compared with ours.

Figure 1: The Auric Layers of a Horse

If you look at Figure 1, you will see that the auric field is thicker and more permeable underneath the stomach, as if there is some kind of a portal there. This is because the top is the consciousness level and the bottom is the subconscious level. The subconscious level is where deep wounding is stored that the animal is not aware of (this happens with humans too). The bottom layer feels and looks to be denser and more like a sponge in texture. Because of this extra sponginess over the stomach area, when you send healing by placing your hands underneath the stomach but not touching it, it seems to penetrate the body more easily.

In sessions I find I spend much of my time sensing the abdomen area, as it can be so revealing. It seems to hold a lot of deep trauma and other emotions in that area. It's as if the wounding is more intense, and they need to protect themselves there. Again, much like humans, it is child-like, with the inner child energy being held in that area, too.

Before I discovered this, I assumed that emotional information would be stored in the heart. If you consider the number of issues some horses have with their stomachs, though, it's not so surprising. Colic starts in the stomach, and if you do dressage, show jumping, hunting, or eventing, you will know that just before you are due to start, your own stomach feels a mess. The horses feel it, too, which is why they have a looser or runnier stool before an event. Those nerves all originate in the stomach!

Abused or Traumatized Animals

If you look at Figure 2, you will see that there is a slight change in the outer layer of the aura. This is the field of an animal that has been severely traumatized or abused at some point in its life. The colors of the aura are more dull, without that shimmery, silver look to them; in fact, it looks more like gray. The trauma shows up as red and rough or uneven. Also notice how the aura changes outward, above the back, like a bubble; this bubble should usually be at the top of the head. This is a soul protection defense mechanism.

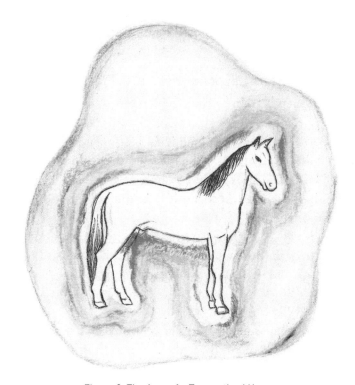

Figure 2: The Aura of a Traumatized Horse

To cope with the trauma, they have shifted their consciousness away from the physical and then have to learn to redefine themselves. If the trauma is severe and is not dealt with, the bubble can detach itself.

The same thing happens in humans when they have experienced deep emotional or physical trauma. As a coping mechanism, they detach themselves during the incident so that they are not entirely present, and afterwards, they may describe it as if they were watching things unfold from another level. In a horse, if emotional, mental, and physical healing all take place, the bow can be shifted back to normal.

Functions of the Aura

As we've now established, horse auras have a similar function and purpose to those of humans, that is, your aura basically describes who you are. The layers of the aura are a blueprint for the cells and tissues that make up the body, as well as for the horse's emotions, state of awareness, relationships, and level of life development. Because diseases and illnesses in the body are reflected in the aura, those who are sensitive can sometimes pick up a problem before it enters the physical body. The aura also has a direct connection to source and receives energy from the surrounding area, too. It then transmits that energy to all parts of the body.

The Layers of the Auric Field

Each layer of the aura can be simple or complex, depending on where the animal is in their level of evolution. The auric layers will also differ from horse to horse, depending on what is happening in their lives at that time. For those that are working horses, the physical (or first level) will be stronger and show a lot of physical ailments, both past and present. Others who are more sensitive and highly strung will have a denser emotional level.

Let's take a look at the levels, starting with the colors. As it is very difficult to illustrate all that happens in the energy field, we have generalized the information and colors for easy understanding.

Colors of the Auric Levels

The colors and shapes of the aura are continually changing, reflecting changes in the horse's physical health, as well as shifts in their emotions and relationships, both with us and within their herd. In general, the colors around horses are shades of pastel—pale blues, greens, purples, and warm yellows like caramel. Even when the color is saturated, it has a shimmery color to it, almost sparkling. The outer soul level particularly has a shimmery, silver-gray look/feel to it.

This is an example of what the different levels of an aura look like:

Figure 3: Personality Zones and Consciousness Levels

Level	Color
Physical	Creamy White
Emotional	Neutral reddish, pink, or caramel
Mental	Ranges of yellow and caramel yellows
Soul	Light pastel blues and greens, sometimes purples and pinks, with a shimmery quality. The final line seen against a background is a silver-gray color.

Physical Level

In the human auric field we would call this the etheric body. It's the first level that emanates from the physical body and has the same shape as the physical body. This etheric (or "physical") layer is like a template of the physical body and reflects what is going on with that body, both inside and outside. It validates that energy is moving through the physical system and indicates the general state of health of the animal.

This is also the area where you can feel the age of the animal. Fairly young animals have a lightness to their energy, whereas much older animals have a heavier, denser feeling to them.

I always do a scan of this layer of the aura. I hold my hands about 10cm above the physical body, working around the outline of the layer to check if there is anything I need to pay attention to there. I look for hot or cold spots and notice any sensations in my body, for example, if my stomach suddenly feels sore. This layer is also where I pick up past or present issues, which may feel like scar tissue or inflammation, respectively.

Once I have identified an area where there may be a problem, I then try to see inside to give me an idea of what is going on. This is called High-Sense Perception and is covered in chapter 6.

If you are a physiotherapist, hydrotherapist, body stress release practitioner, or kinesiologist, or you read animals or work with them physically in any other way, this is where you will be able to pick up a physical condition, sometimes even before it manifests in the physical body. I have often heard these types of practitioners say that they just know something is going on in a certain area, even though there is no physical proof, like a limp, for example.

In my experience, if you are trained in a medical field, for example as a nurse, doctor, or vet, or you simply have a background in anatomy, then the etheric layer will be the one from which you can most easily pick up information. Otherwise, you will be going about it the hard way, as I do: seeing something, then having to research it to try and understand exactly what it means. I am constantly learning new things and about areas in the body I never knew existed. Biology in school doesn't come close.

Emotional Level

The emotional layer is usually a very neutral pink-red color, and blobs of other colors also come up here, which tell us more about what is going on in the emotional level. Animal communicators read this level naturally, because we connect with animals through the heart chakra. Most animals can manipulate, or cloak, the color, though, depending on what they want you to see.

An animal communicator may feel an emotion but not be quite sure what it is. Sometimes an animal mentions an episode in their life, but does so very briefly. They are only willing to tell you that something happened and that it scared them emotionally. In that case, either they have already dealt with it and feel it is not necessary to reveal all, or it was so traumatic that they don't feel ready to show a human just yet, or maybe ever. This is perfectly fine, as forcing an issue might just make matters worse. When they are ready, and if they feel they want to, then they might share a trauma at a later stage.

Sometimes animals find it hard to express what they feel and will therefore try to convey it through the animal communicator's body. This is the way I pick up emotions, and I then have to try and put into words what I am feeling. That can be extremely difficult, and I often get a range of emotions that are so deep and intense that I battle to associate the feeling with the correct word.

The emotional level shows the emotional health of the animal. A light color shows a positive attitude, and a dark color, like gray, a negative or depressed emotional space. Usually the darker the color, the more intense the emotion.

CASE STUDY: Patch and the Tokai Baboons

I was working with a horse named Patch in a yard on the edge of Tokai Forest in Cape Town. As the session was closing, a huge troop of baboons started moving through the yard and the field next door, all foraging away and playing happily. The troop moves through the paddocks about once a week and are always watched by the baboon monitors, who make sure they don't cause trouble in the nearby residential area. My next client appointment was only in an hour, so I had time on my hands and sat down on the edge of the paddock to watch them, enjoying this unexpected treat.

About 15 minutes later, a male baboon started chasing a female carrying a baby, which does sometimes happen. This carried on for a while until he finally caught up with her and attacked the baby. The rest of the males immediately ran to her rescue and chased the aggressive male away.

This all took place very close to where Patch was grazing with a friend. At the time, they simply moved off, showing no sign of real distress, and carried on grazing a few meters away. The troop calmed down, and half an hour later my session with Patch started.

As usual, I began with the floral oil but was somewhat surprised by his selection. He showed a strong interest in rose then violet leaf, even choosing to lick the violet leaf off my hand, very slowly. Violet leaf is for anxiety and nervousness, and rose can be used to counteract trauma.

I then scanned his energetic field doing an auric body scan to guide me as to what to offer next and found that his emotional body was pulsating and spiky, which was very unusual. He moved away as soon as he had showed me what was going on, as if he was uncomfortable. I gave him a few minutes, then simply sent calming energy to him, after which he settled again and I carried on with the oils.

Another oil offered for trauma is arnica, and he licked about 100ml from my hand—again very slowly and making sure he got oil on both the front and the back of his tongue (there are receptors in the back of the tongue). After that his emotional field was still pulsating but the spikes were starting to settle.

Momma Baboon Showing Us Her Baby

The baboon mother with the injured baby appeared in the middle of the session, and sat holding her baby about two meters away from us. She was showing us the infant was hurt. At first I did not realize that she was trying to get my attention (or that the baby was hurt) and carried on working, but when she did not move off, I turned, looked at her fully and realized that the baby was injured and she wanted help. She knew humans could intervene and help, and it certainly looked quite bad. I then immediately called one of the baboon monitors, who was walking behind the troop as they were on the move again.

He radioed and let whoever was in charge know what had happened. As soon as he had finished, she moved off with the rest of the troop, mission accomplished.

Patch was also very concerned about whether the little one would make it, and asked if we humans would intervene and help the baby, as we do with horses. It was a question I couldn't answer as I just didn't know. So I asked his owner to follow up about the little one with the baboon monitor next time the troop passed through, and to pass the news on to Patch.

To watch a video of this episode see here:

https://www.youtube.com/watch?v=Xiyv88xmxHc

Title: Male juvenile baboon chasing a mom and her baby

Figure 4: Patch's Emotional Layer after the Baboon Incident

Mental Level

This layer reflects the mental state of an animal, indicating their thinking, rationality, intelligence, cheerfulness, and optimism. The more highly evolved the animal, the more pronounced the color. When connecting to horses on this level, it's possible to get a feel for things, such as what they are afraid of and their likes and dislikes. It is also on this level that they communicate with the rest of the world.

The mental layer lies above the personality area and is mostly yellow in color with some greens. This area reflects some of their personality and problem-solving abilities, both of which can vary widely from animal to animal. Some animals have a very dry sense of humor, while others love playing jokes on their humans and are quite cocky and cheeky. There are also those who are quite serious, and others who never stop talking and enjoy a good gossip. We look at some different personality types in more detail below.

Perceiving this layer particularly helps with working horses and issues around training or jumping and so on. In an animal communication session, it allows an open interaction around any confusion or mis-communication that is going on between the human and the animal. Sometimes, as humans, we are not clear at all about what we want from our animals. We tend to say one thing but mean something else, or even change our minds while thinking about a problem.

For example, let's say you own a horse and do show jumping. Your horse clears all the other jumps but is hesitant at a particular one or on a turn, maybe even passing it by. At the end of the round, you are unhappy as you cannot understand why he didn't want to go over that jump. Is it possible that it is the one jump that you are hesitant about and don't particularly like? Horses pick up on our emotions, so if you were slightly fearful of a complicated jump, your horse would have picked up on your anxiety and listened to what you were unintentionally communicating to him: to avoid that one. If an animal receives mixed messages, it's not surprising if they become confused.

Especially if you are working with animals in a competitive manner, you need to stay very aware of what you think and feel around them. Be clear and concise about want you want them to do, and show them in your mind's eye what you would like. Remember, they are telepathic.

Soul Level

When reading an animal telepathically or picking up on their aura, it is through the soul level that you can perceive their level of consciousness, that is, how evolved they are in their spiritual path and belief system. This does not mean that one is better or less than the other. It is simply that they sometimes display their level of spiritual advancement in the way they communicate and interact with us and each other.

In general, the soul level reflects the will of the animal and their divine connection to both the universe and to a higher purpose. It is a high frequency of energy that also holds the entire field together.

In older souls, the spiritual layer of the aura is denser and thicker, and it's as if you can instantly feel it in every part of your body. The intensity of the connection sometimes overwhelms me and then I need to just ride it out physically and emotionally until I feel able to continue. In an older, wiser, more evolved soul, the bridge between the physical and spiritual has been built; it always hovers above the solar plexus, as in Figure 5.

The soul level shows all the colors within the aura, and if the colors here are light, then there is a sense of calm. When the colors are darker and the bow above the head is out of place, then it reflects trauma of some kind (see Figure 2).

Figure 5: Soul Evolvement Level

Soul Evolvement

With horses, there is a definite step-by-step developmental process that takes place over a period of time. If you look at Figures 3 and 5, you will notice a triangle that links the third eye, throat chakra, and the star of the soul (see more about the chakras in the next chapter):

1. Horses and other animals are born with heart energy, but they need to experience life, just as we do, in order to gain a greater understanding of the world and people around them. The heart chakra is to do with love and in horses takes the form of the star of the soul.

2. The throat chakra is about expression of their personality, and in younger teen horses, you may pick up a cockiness about them here as they establish their rank.

3. The third eye has to do with destiny and is the last chakra to be activated.

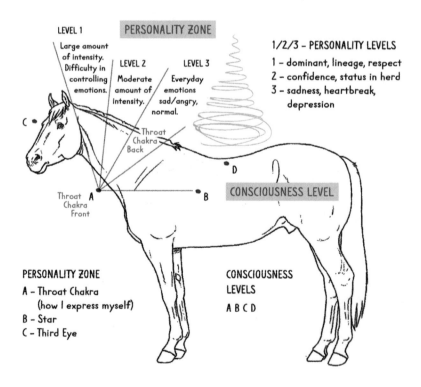

Figure 6: Personality Levels

A horse might only have the first two levels activated in a lifetime. The more evolved the animal, the more the interaction and communication among these three chakras, as their various levels of awareness are each consciously mastered and then come together. This raises their vibration, and especially when the third eye comes in, it moves them up on the spiral to a higher level of consciousness.

In the next chapter we will look at chakras in greater detail, including where they are and how they work.

When working with a horse, I have often felt certain areas to be non-active. For example, a young five-year-old horse I recently worked with had no energy whatsoever in his heart area. This doesn't mean that he doesn't have a heart or doesn't feel anything; it just means that he needs to work on it. Right now, he is at a stage of his life where he is full of himself. He is an absolute stunner who I am sure will go far in the jumping circle, but he has no emotional connection to his owner or anyone else who rides him. This will affect his jumping career and the growth of his consciousness. It is one of the reasons he is here, to learn this particular aspect.

I tried to get things to begin moving on an energetic level, so this developmental stage could be speeded up a little and his heart chakra activated. Being shut down in the heart area has consequences, and for this horse in particular, if he doesn't settle down and stop showing off, he will be sold and might suffer heartache at losing his friends and the stunning yard he will need to leave behind. On the other hand, if he can learn to open up his heart and give the gift of love, he will receive it in return, much like humans.

The Spiritual Cord

As humans in the womb, we are attached to our mothers via an umbilical cord. When we are born this cord is cut, and we are then completely on our own physically. We still have a spiritual umbilical cord that connects us to the spiritual realm, though. The existence of this energetic cord has been described and documented over thousands of years. When it is time for us to leave the physical, this cord is severed and the soul departs the body, moving up and out.

The same thing happens with animals but in a different way. The spiral you see in the picture below is a bridge to the spiritual realm, and it shifts and moves as the animal grows. Young foals are born with this spiral flowing downward, toward the ground, until they are broken in or become adults. As they become aware of their purpose and begin to understand their place in the greater whole, it starts rising from the belly button upward.

In older horses, it can often be seen tapering upward toward the heavens, as they connect with their divinity and their higher path. Although it doesn't always appear in older animals, the more conscious and evolved they are, the more tangibly it can be felt in their fields. Timelines are shown to me in this area, indicating their stage of development and how conscious they are of divine energy.

Figure 7: A Foal with a Spiritual Cord

Personality Levels

The personality levels have to do with how an animal projects themselves to the world. This is the energy they use to control the first impression another animal or a human would get from them.

Horses connect from the heart level, but show will from the physical level when they think that it influences their status in a herd environment. This especially applies to their lineage, as it is very important to them who their sire and dam (mother) are.

Most of us know who our mother and father are. Horses do, too, even if their father came out of a test tube. Whenever I do readings on competitive horses, whether in the fields of show jumping, dressage, or cross country, they always bring up who their parents are and how that fact automatically gives them a certain status in the horse community and in the herd. As you can see in Figure 8, the personality level starts from the base of the mane and ends between the ears.

Figure 8: Location of the Personality Level

In the throat and neck area there are two chakras: one at the front of the throat and one at the back of the neck. The personality levels are found within the back of the throat chakra. Within that personality layer, three different levels of emotion are found.

LEVEL 1: In this level, there is a large amount of emotional intensity, which can include feelings like intense heartbreak, grief, or depression. In times of stress and trauma, it is difficult to control these emotions.

LEVEL 2: Here there is a moderate amount of emotional intensity, as if the dial has been turned up. There are strong feelings, but the animal is still in control.

LEVEL 3: The first level is where there is a normal amount of emotional intensity. Emotions are present, and it's okay to feel angry or sad.

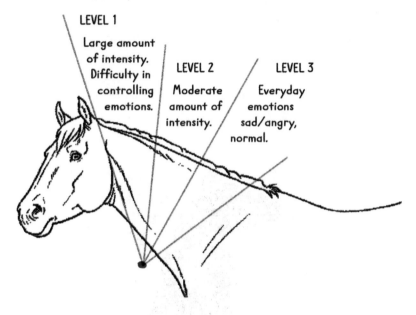

Figure 9: Layers of the Personality Level

CASE STUDY: What Is Up, Santa?

Something was wrong with Santa, a beautiful 15-year old chestnut. He wasn't his usual cheerful self, and his owner knew something was bothering him. Although he appeared to be fine physically, he seemed to have lost his zest for life. He didn't greet her like he usually did, his head hung on outrides, and he seemed depressed. She connected with me to find out what was wrong.

I did the reading telepathically. When I connected to him, I had an overwhelming sense of absolute grief wash over me. It took me a while to try and adjust to this energy as it was so profound, and I actually cried the tears he was feeling. A good 20 minutes into the session, when I had managed to set my emotions aside and finally carry on with the session, he explained that he had recently lost a soul friend. Santa had been rescued a few months previously at the very last minute. He was on his way to be put down when Trudi, his owner, stepped in and rescued him and said she would look after him. At the time, he had been terribly thin and malnourished. Cocky, a bay with a blaze had been there from the day he entered his new yard. Cocky had supported him emotionally as his health and faith in humanity slowly returned. When he woke up in the morning and looked out of his stable, the first thing he saw was his friend Cocky. They became such good friends that they shared a paddock and spent every moment together.

Unfortunately, the time came when Cocky had to be put down due to old age. Although everyone knew it was coming it was still a shock, and Santa was absolutely devastated at the loss of his friend. Although he understood the passing, he still missed him physically not being there.

As the saying goes, time heals. It took a good few weeks for him to get over the loss, but he eventually did and was back to his old happy self again, greeting his owner the minute she got out of her car and being the affectionate fellow he was before.

Do animals feel intense emotions like we do? Without a doubt! And that intensity of emotions would come from the heart area and the Level 1 on Figure 9. If you were doing an auric scan you could possibly feel the intensity in your heart, and when scanning Level 1 you would pick it up there, too.

Santa

Personality Types

When doing a reading on any animal, as the session progresses I often get a sense of their personalities. Their little quirks and sense of humor always come out, and so do their food preferences, as these are extremely important in any animal's life.

Some tend to be quite serious and feel that their role in the household is a very important one. There are those who are very talkative and want to be acknowledged, understood, and heard. Then there are some who are quite sensitive and shy or more anxious and nervous.

While recording our sessions with horses, I noticed that the personality of the horse would almost always be reflected in a certain area, either from the top of the neck downward or from the start of the neck up to the ears. It also seemed that the stronger and more dominant the personality, the stronger the flow of energy and the brighter the color.

The personality area also reflects what is going on in the back throat chakra on the mane. This makes sense, as the throat chakra is not just about voicing; it's also to do with their place in the greater universe, which comes from their heritage and their lineage, and everything that goes with that. With very difficult animals, I would always start working with the (front) throat chakra, as it is easiest to access purely from a physical aspect and closest to the heart chakra, and then move them to the back chakra. The heart chakra seems to have a supportive influence on the throat chakra. Once I feel that the energy has shifted—meaning it's become lighter and freer flowing as opposed to heavy when you first feel it and there is a problem—I then move to the back throat chakra.

A Dominant Personality

In Figure 10, you can see a more dominant ego, the type of personality usually found in any competitive field involving horses, such as show jumping, dressage, or cross country. These horses tend to have a certain presence that demands attention and admiration, a bit like a typical teen showing off to his peers. They may love showing off or enjoy a good gossip about daily life in the stables. The more dominant and confident they are, the more likely it is that their personality energy is very much in the third level, as in, "I am the matriarch. Thou shalt bow to me." This feeling of importance is often determined by their lineage, and also by the respect they have from their peers and the people around them. As a result, they can be very arrogant and difficult to control.

Figure 10: Aura of a Dominant Personality

A Confident and Empowered Personality

The confidence area defines how a horse comes across. It looks like a fan and can move around. For example, when they are confident and feeling empowered, it flares out. They feel their higher status and have greater awareness and more interactions within the herd. If there is a fall from grace, however, it moves downward.

Some horses are missing the fan completely, which indicates trauma. They have shut down a certain level of consciousness in order to cope. This might happen, for instance, if a mare has lost a foal, either because it died or was taken away too early.

Figure 11: Aura of a Confident and Empowered Personality

A Proud Personality

Here you can see the pride and energy of the horse. Pride can appear in various forms and is often related to who they are or what they have accomplished. For example, they may be proud of the foal they have had or they may have won plenty of rosettes during their career.

Figure 12: Aura of a Proud Personality

A Gentle Personality

Here is a more gentle and easy-going spirit, who has a balanced outlook on life and is okay with everything around them.

I am sure I will be able to add a few more personality types to this chapter as I learn about them over the years. For now, I hope this information will at least help you to understand how a personality is displayed in the aura.

Figure 13: Aura of a Gentle, Loving, and Easy-Going Personality

Cat Energy Fields or Aura

We now know that everything has an energy field. We have looked at auras, chakras, a horse's aura, and now we will be taking a look at a cat's aura.

The basic aura is the same for both cats and dogs, as far as the different levels of the aura and the colors are concerned. There are subtle differences in the way they communicate with us and with each other, and we will look at this more in depth under each species.

Cat auras appear wider than those of horses. There is also more of a focus around the head, which begins to expand, going up from the shoulder blades and chest area. It shows more personality. That does not mean to say other animals don't have a strong personality; it simply means that cats express their personalities in the upper layer of the body. It also looks smoother than a horse's; a horse's aura is chunkier in looks. The transition between the different layers is smoother and not as defined; they blend into each other. The colors also appear to be more in hues. The average height of a cat's aura is about 40 cm above them, so definitely bigger than horses.

Figure 14: Auric Field of a Cat

Personality Section

With cats, there is no definite area of the body where we can pinpoint exactly where the personality lies, as in horses. A horse's personality field is far more structured than a cat's. With cats, the personality is displayed in the second layer of the aura. It is displayed from the shoulders down.

The more dominant a cat's personality, the more the color appears to be bigger and brighter around the head, as they put more energy into that area and display it to others.

Cats hold their personalities in their energy fields and manipulate the mental field to show off their personality, if they so wish. Cats have a tendency to suppress their energy around their stomach, even if they don't always want to let us see it or touch it. For instance, the aura is extended when they are curious, and the mental layer becomes brighter if they want to explore more. It's as if they use their aura as an extrasensory perception tool to see if it is worth getting up to go and investigate further.

Cats reflect their personalities by changing their auras. Examples include:

- **Hiding cat, aloof and cautious:** Projects a less powerful or forced aura than others.

- **Confident cat:** Layers of the aura expand and are thicker (*I am*). Shows off the energy field ("look at me").

- **Curious cat:** Tail going left or right, energy moves forward ("hello" if you are new to the house).

Cat Tails

We all know that by looking at a cat's body language and tail, it can reveal how the cat is feeling. It gives us an indication of their mood and emotions. In the illustration below, you can see the cat's tail has a small bend in it, close to the top.

Have you ever noticed how, when you arrive at a new house or place where cats are living, the cats will sometimes come into the room and sus you out? They have a good look at you and their tails are flicking at the same time, usually from left to right. They first are reading you energetically and then saying hello by flicking their tail. It all depends on the individual cat. Some cats are very friendly and will go up to any stranger with the tail up in the air saying hello; others are far more reserved or timid and then you have to work a little harder to get such a tail-flicking welcome.

Emotional Layer

The emotional layer is bigger in kittens than the mental layer. They need more engagement with humans in order to develop the mental level.

Cats are more mentally evolved; dogs are more emotionally evolved. That does not mean to say that either way is better or more advanced; it simply is how they were created and how they function. The more they interact with humans the more the heart chakra opens and expands. Because they are more mentally evolved, they are more adept at manipulating mental energy.

CASE STUDY: Understanding Sebastian

Sebastian is a Burmese cat recently up for adoption as his elderly parents moved into a retirement home and they could not take him with them. He was adopted by Maryse, Andrew, and their two boys. They own a gorgeous South African ridgeback, a miniature dachshund, and another female cat, Jinx, a snowshoe Siamese who is very bossy and dominant.

Sebastian really battled to settle down, and for the first month hardly left the bedroom vanity drawer. He would come out at night and spend some telly time with the family at night, but otherwise remained in the bedroom in that drawer. He had been with the family a month now and was still afraid of everything. He was also petrified of the vacuum cleaner. Things could not go on like this, so I was called in.

I decided to do the session in the lounge as I was there in the day but it was still out of his comfort zone and away from the bedroom. First I had a chat with Monty, the Ridgeback, as he is head of the household and that needs to be respected. I politely explained how Sebastian came to stay with them; then I asked if he could please try and refrain from chasing the cats as I was sure he would understand that Sebastian was still trying to settle in. Monty has a lovely deep voice and immediately felt sorry for Sebastian. He reassured me that he would really try not to chase him. The other cat, yes, because he was downright cheeky, thought he owned the house and looked down on Monty, and he could not have that happening. Did I realize he had a job to do and had to keep order in the household? But right oh'...he was on board. The dachshund was no problem—she loves everyone and everything. Sebastian was fetched from the room and anxiously settled onto someone's lap, eyes as wide as saucers and wanting to run.

I immediately started with the oils. I was sitting on the floor with Sebastian, so was able to watch his face and his body. He immediately selected rose, violet leaf, and yarrow. Yarrow is for trauma. After three minutes with yarrow and a very slight yawn, he started purring very slightly. We had a talk about various things, and one of them was the vacuum cleaner.

Sebastian

He simply stated that he hated it. He said that it looked like a flying saucer from another planet and politely asked that when any vacuuming was on the cards to please leave a cupboard ajar so that he could escape to that. If there was a box in it, even better. Once the "flying saucer" had left he would come out and go back to wherever he had been. I discussed it with Maryse, who immediately agreed, and that's exactly what the arrangement has been for the last few months and everyone is happy. The days following the session, Sebastian is like a different cat. He has gained confidence and now leaves the room and explores the house.

Sometimes we want animals to embrace and accept things for what they are—a vacuum cleaner, a blender, and so on; but that is a bit unfair, as we all have things we don't like or are afraid of. So work around it. Accept that it's not going to change. Make an arrangement that suits everyone.

Figure 15: A Tear in the Heart Center

The above image shows a cat we noticed at a rescue centre, who at one point moved close to us and deliberately showed us his field. His heart chakra had a tear in it, causing a leak in his heart chakra to develop and energy to flow over the breast bone as he was taken away from his mother too soon. When I acknowledged him and started stroking him he began kneading the grass which brought a sense of belonging in this instance.

Stalking

Nothing is nicer than watching a cat preparing to stalk something, whether it be a toy or something it considers prey. Cats stalk as part of their hunting routine. They seem to suddenly become very focused on the prey objects, then the body starts moving in anticipation of the pounce. If they focus and watch while prepping the physical body, it saves them time and energy.

Here is what happens in their energy field while stalking. The first layer of the field (the physical layer) compacts, and instead of being more spongelike and flowing, it becomes solid and dense as the energy changes.

The emotional layer slightly thickens, but the mental layer gradually becomes more solid and dense and then starts spiking in anticipation just before the pounce or leap. It is a very pretty thing to observe in the field as it is so bright and colorful.

Figure 16: Milly Stalking Another Cat

How Cats Communicate

We have identified two things that happen when cats communicate with each other. First, they detect each other's energy fields. If there is a group of cats or more than one cat, they communicate with each other just like we do. Second, they communicate via pheromones (hormones) and not visibly.

In Figure 17, you can see the individual energy fields and how they connect with the cat's consciousness around them. They are able to extend their fields in almost the same way a spider builds a web.

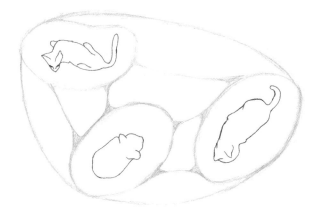

Figure 17: Group of Cats' Collective Consciousness

Pheromone Contact

When cats are in a group they release a type of pheromone to communicate with each other. Pheromones are chemical substances that animals release in an environment. At times, it is visible. Just like horses, a cat will lift their upper lips back to expose the upper part of the gum, sniff, and hold the mouth slightly open to inhale cat pheromones within the group of cats. Tiny ducts connect them to openings behind the cat's teeth in the roof of the mouth. It is known as the Flehmen response, a German word that means "lip curl." This might be mistaken for an aggressive snarl but is perfectly normal and peaceful cat behavior. Cats have pheromone-producing glands in several parts of their bodies:

- In the perineal area – used for marking territory and signaling purposes.

- On the paw pads – used to tell other cats they were there, how long ago, their mood, and their intentions in marking.

- Glands in the cheeks – released by rubbing on something or greeting someone in a friendly manner and also to mark familiar objects. Cheek pheromones rubbed against objects can tell other cats that they are friendly or that the territory is owned. It's a sign of true affection if your feline companion bestows this on you. Pheromones in urine notify other cats if the cat is intact or fixed and whether a boy or a girl.

They also seem to be able to detect pheromones by keeping the mouth closed. The sense of smell travels into the nose and then seems to enter into those pheromone receptors in the upper lip. On a physical level, it has a sweet vinegar/chemical taste and can be felt starting on either side of the upper gum and in the side of the mouth.

Cat Auric Scan

This is the cat auric scan of a cat named Tigger. The top of the head area reveals how he was when we started the session and he was very stand-offish toward me. Wanted to know who I was and why I was there, and generally thought I was way below him, like most humans in his life. When I did an auric scan, I offered rose for issues of the heart, and as you can see, it immediately activated the heart and got the energy flowing. This helped him to relax more and to accept me. The trauma in the tail is from when someone stood on his tail. He is very sensitive about his tail.

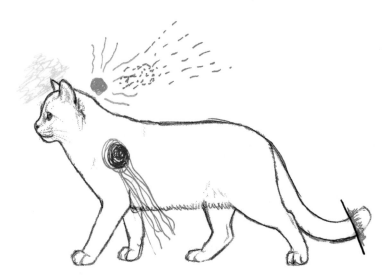

Figure 18: Cat Auric Scan

CASE STUDY: Fabio – Grief

Fabio and Tino shared a home and were brothers in spirit, always together through thick and thin. They were together for about four years when one day Tino decided to chase a bird across the road and was hit by a car. He passed away in his mom Heidi's arms. Needless to say the weeks after his passing were extremely painful for

44

Heidi and Fabio as they battled to adjust, grieving the loss of Tino. Fabio followed his mom everywhere, he cried for his brother and lost physical condition.

Heidi is a kinesiologist and possesses a wide range of essential oils. She bought a new lemon oil that she offered to Fabio when getting home. Upon sniffing the oil he started meowing for the first time in ages. His eyes brightened, his body shifted and he became more alert. He then started investigating areas that his deceased brother had claimed as his own and rolled in the shelf where Tino had slept (he never did this before).

Fabio

I had distilled some rose water which I had given to Heidi to offer to Fabio. She said Fabio could not get enough of it. He lapped it up and wanted it applied onto his fur, then rolled onto his back for tickles to his tummy. His eyes brightened and his tail became more upright, more bounce overall. Several days later I called in and once again we offered him the rose water - he inhaled deeply then moved his body so that it could be applied to his solar plexus too.

In the days that followed Fabio once again became the boy Heidi knew; his physical appearance improved, he started interacting more with people and generally seemed happier.

While Tino will never be forgotten, the lemon oil and rose hydro-sol helped Fabio through the griefing process and brought healing.

Gifts

This is a sensitive subject that gets brought up in nearly every session that I do with a cat. People want to know and understand why a domesticated cat will bring "gifts" to their owners in the form of a kill they have made, such as a pigeon, a mouse, or a lizard. Some cats bring their owners leaves or sticks. The cat can be very vocal and may even howl, announcing his gift until the owner notices. Many people find this horrific and scold the cat instead of understanding why the cat has gifted them with something.

This pattern of behavior is natural for a cat, so scolding your cat for something that lies in their very nature is not helpful. Having said that, there are some cats who genuinely enjoy a good squeal from their owner for their own enjoyment, and for this reason repeat the behavior.

Cats do have a very dry sense of humor and love a good laugh and joke, especially if it is at someone else's expense. If you think your cat might be one of them (watch their face closely and see if you can see a smirk of satisfaction, that will be a clue). I suggest you change your reaction to the offering and try to force a smile, not say a word, then dispose of the carcass.

As a human, we know how it feels when we buy a gift for someone and they don't have the manners to say thank you. It's rude, and you feel your time and effort are unappreciated. Cats also think that. Why should it be any different?

From a nutritional point of view, there is a very valid reason why cats instinctively hunt and eat their prey. Cats need more protein than dogs, and if they don't get it in their diet, from food we provide, they will source it from nature.

There are two main ingredients found in meat:

1. Arachidonic acid
2. Taurine – an essential amino acid found in meat and fish

Taurine-deficient cats will often exhibit signs of depression, shortness of breath, and this deficiency can lead to a host of other things.In the wild, cats hunt mice, rabbits, and birds. Like all carnivores, they devour the stomach contents of their prey, thereby eating fruit, nuts, and eggs. If your cat catches prey and eats it, then he is simply supplementing his diet.

If your cat attempts to catch prey and then play with it, not sure of what to do with it, praise him or her and take it away. Remember life is all about learning, and they simply have not yet mastered the necessary skill to kill and eat it. It is extremely difficult to try and get a cat to stop this type of behavior. Sometimes, we can negotiate with them and the owner. They might want raw meat or protein added to their diet (not necessarily daily but once a week) or even fish.

Whenever I bury something that was once a living creature, I say a prayer that my mom wrote, as it is a ritual that seems to comfort me, and I get to acknowledge the life the animal had on Earth. I am happy to share it with you.

"Ashes to ashes, dust to dust,
Thank you, dear animal, for sharing your life with us.
Go back to your creator, from whence you came.
Your life is over now, ready to begin again."

Dog Energy Fields or Aura

As with cats, a dog's personality is reflected more in the head area. The more distinguished the breed, the more evident the personality will be in this area of the body.

A dog's aura looks similar to that of a horse. The spacing above the head is bigger and wider, with the auric layers spaced around every 10cm. The bigger and higher the auric level around the head, the more intelligent the dog. Working dogs, such as border collies and beagles, or a mixed breed that has to think or actively work, such as the dogs at the airport, will have a much bigger mental area around the head than a normal dog. That does not mean to say the average dog doesn't think. Of course they do, but they are more leisurely about it.

Dogs appear to be more emotionally evolved due to their work with humans. Their communication is more primal and follows instinct and is less controlled. The more domesticated the dog, the more the energy shifts to the front of the body and from the heart area. The personality will be reflected more in the head area and be shown to us.

The outer layer is more porous and receptive to outside influences. It looks and behaves very much like a sponge when the dog is typically greeting someone they know and love, with the heart chakra opening. The saying that a dog loves you more than you love yourself is so true, as the minute they see someone they love, their hearts shine and the heart chakra is activated. With other animals, we need to work a little harder to have this happen instantaneously.

Figure 19: Typical Canine Aura

The physical level of a dog's energy field is thinner around the hips and over the tail and bum area and is not as equal all around as it is with horses. They distribute their energy more toward the front of their bodies than toward the hip area. The field then becomes bigger again around the tail. The appearance and texture is smooth. Aura size is dependent on the personality of the dog, but extends about 30 cm outward in healthy dogs. The area around the stomach is more equal than horses and cats.

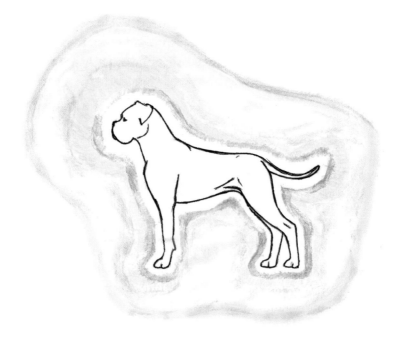

Figure 20: Side View of the Dog Aura

Certain breeds are very aware of themselves. In their minds they have a lineage, and that is important to them. Bassett hounds may think of themselves as superior and entitled and have more presence than another type of dog, such as an Africanis (the name for all Southern African native dogs – a mix of anything and everything you can imagine). That is reflected in the area above their heads and their hearts. A lot of energy can be seen around the seat of the soul.

If you have ever lived with a dog, then you know how expressive their tail can be. There is a lot of energy around it, as it is part of the way dogs communicate with each other and show how they feel. When dogs greet each other, their energy shifts to the tail—they put more information about themselves near the bum. When they bark, the energy moves near the head.

How Dogs Communicate

Dogs communicate with each other in a variety of ways. We know that one way they communicate with us humans is by using their body language, and if you live with a dog you quickly learn to read your dog's body language, just like they do ours. We also learn to differentiate between their different barks—how a "hello" bark sounds compared to a deep growl of "I am frightened" or "Someone unknown is outside." This is how they communicate with each other and what happens in their energy fields.

Barking

Remember the energy field is constantly flowing and moving, so when a dog barks that field of energy shifts from the tail upward to the head, projecting the energy from the middle of the body. They put all of their energy into one thing at a time.

Butt Sniffing and Lineage Presentation

Dogs love to sniff another dog's nether regions. It's often something people get embarrassed about, but if they were dogs, they would realize just how much information the dog is picking up about other dogs and have a better understanding.

When we meet someone new, we look at their appearance. Do they have brown hair? Is it long or short? Do they look Italian or Egyptian? Do they have brown eyes, long ears, and so on? We also feel each other out energetically without knowing it. I am sure you have met someone and instantly liked or disliked the person. You are not sure why, but something just feels off. We take this information in through our eyes and how we feel.

Dogs do that, too, but 90 percent of that information comes from sniffing the bum area. They can immediately tell how old the other dog is, what they last ate, whether they are male or female, have been neutered or have a litter, the type of home they live in, and a million other snippets of information. Now if you could tell all this information by sniffing around the lower tail area without mentioning a word, would you not also do it?

When two new dogs come into contact, say hello, and present themselves nose to bum, they are communicating with each other. A large amount of energy shifts to the tail in order to put more info near the bum (This is me, who I am, what I am, and how I live).

They do this when they want to show off their lineage to another dog (I am a German Shepherd) and so on. See Figure 21 for a visual presentation of this area.

Figure 21: Canine Butt Sniffing and Lineage Presentation
NOTE: The line indicates the area from which the dog presents its lineage.

Dog Language

Dogs adapt their language to humans, so often, when doing a reading, I would get a certain type of accent and would be able to tell if a dog came from a different country and spoke a different language, such as German. I don't know how to speak German but can recognize a German accent. Sometimes, it comes up at the start of the session, but more often than not, the information, in a language I cannot speak, comes in toward the middle or the end of the session. It is something I have always wondered about. Why then? Over a period of time, I began to see (and confirmed it when working with Melana) that the dog adapts their language to humans. Because I am actively involved with the human in session now, the language being used at that time comes through. I am in South Africa so I often speak English and Afrikaans in a session, because either the owner is English and the dog was previously with Afrikaans owners, or vice versa.

That happens at the start of the session because I am fluent in both languages. It's the foreign languages that take time. It makes for some interesting sessions, as sometimes a word or a sentence in another language carries more meaning and understanding in the way it comes through.

Figure 22: Dog Showing Off Their Sex

The spirals at the back get projected to other dogs. In this case there are two spirals which signify a female. One spiral would indicate that it is a male. This spiral usually gets projected before they physically come in contact with each other, or when speaking telepathically.

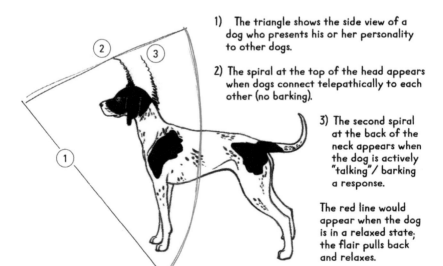

1) The triangle shows the side view of a dog who presents his or her personality to other dogs.

2) The spiral at the top of the head appears when dogs connect telepathically to each other (no barking).

3) The second spiral at the back of the neck appears when the dog is actively "talking"/ barking a response.

The red line would appear when the dog is in a relaxed state; the flair pulls back and relaxes.

Figure 23: Dog Personality and Communication

Dogs can talk to each other or to us, they cannot do both at the same time. They need to prioritize who to speak to—either the human or other dogs. When playing with other dogs, their attention is solely on the other dog, not on the human.

Figure 24: Dog Instating Personality and Dominancy
The bubble above the head is a personality check on the etheric level.
She is forcing her dominancy onto people in alpha mode.

Figure 25: Front View of a Dog's Listening

That can be a problem on walks when a dog thinks it's a human. All its energy is projected toward humans and not enough is projected toward other dogs, which then leaves the nether region energetically exposed. No defense and weak in that area. Or another dog rushes up from behind with the good idea to sniff and say hello, but the rush is miscommunicated, the dog on the leash feels exposed, and you did not ask permission. This could lead to dog fights, which happen out of the blue when another dog who is more dominant might reprimand your dog, saying "You think you are better than us" (that is, more human) and take a nip.

Sometimes when dogs bark, all that they are doing is talking to you, not fighting with you, as in "I am asking you to listen." We all know people who love to talk a lot. Well, there are dogs who also like to talk a lot. One of them is my bassett hound, who gives an opinion on everything by barking. We often speak telepathically, but when she feels adamant about something she barks.

There is always a reason for a dog to be barking. Just listening to the type of barking can tell us a lot about what is going on. If alone all day for hours and never walked, that dog would bark out of loneliness and frustration, and you will be able to pick that up by the tone of the bark. A welcome home bark or yelp is the best in the world; it sounds happy.

Pack Communication

With cats, we saw the web effect; with dogs, it's the cloud effect. Living in Africa, we often get afternoon clouds rolling in. When you watch a ball of clouds move like that, it is exactly how a pack will communicate with each other. It starts with the first bark (first cloud), then carries on rolling until the cloud is past and everyone is silent again and the necessary information has reached all recipients.

Overshadowing Shield

Have you ever watched two dogs close to each other, one barking a lot and the other calm and collected, unperturbed by the other dog's barking? What very often happens is the calm and collected dog cloaks the aura of the other dog. If they feel they are misbehaving, they tell them so ("come now, stand down"), and they push the field down, subduing or suppressing it. This can happen when one dog is also stressed out and another reassures it.

I have tried the above with dogs, cats, and horses numerous times, when I feel they are nervous or anxious. When it is done with love and compassion, they respond incredibly well.

I have also suggested it to clients when there is a male dominancy issue as a way to keep the offender in check and prevent fighting. In a case like that, the human would imagine their energy field going over the animal's with a more dominant assertive energy. Remember that when a dominancy issue is occurring, there is usually an underlying sense of fear or insecurity. So you force your field on theirs without moving at all (you don't have to) and literally "hug" them with your field.

Remember, too, that your emotions will be passed over to them through the field, so if you do this, have your emotions under control and be sure you are not stressed or nervous, as they will pick it up. They seem to quickly get the message and back off if you catch it early enough. It's just like swaddling a baby. You give a verbal clue in a calm voice and then follow that with your energetic shield. You are saying, "Everything is fine. You are safe."

Figure 26: Dog Energetic Reassurance to Each Other

New dogs have to learn the language of the new household, which is why it can take a while to figure out the pack language.

If you have a new cat or dog coming into your home, please tell them what is happening—that you would like to take them home, describe your home, and mention the animals you have in your home (if any). The same applies to the animals you already have at home. Describe the other animal so that they get curious and look forward to meeting the newcomer, and mention you want them to be part of the family.

Rafiki

CASE STUDY: Rafiki – Anxiety

As you can see, Rafiki is a beautiful German Shepherd. I was called out to her home that she shares with her brother due to severe sep-aration anxiety issues she was experiencing when her owners left for work. The owners have security cameras in place and noticed over the last few months that every time they left for work, she would bark and cry for a long period of time all along the fence. The neighbors also mentioned it, so they decided to get me in for help. In session,

Rafiki told me that there had been a major change in the household a few months ago that deeply upset her: one of her favorite humans was no longer with them. She missed her terribly as she had been there throughout the day and kept the dogs company. Now that she was no longer there, it caused Rafiki a huge amount of stress when her owners left for work as she was worried they might not come back, just like the other human had not come back.

It turned out that about three months ago the maid, who had been there for several years and whom Rafiki had known since she was a puppy, had been fired for stealing. It was the maid she was missing and when her owners left in the morning now, it felt like she was being abandoned. This caused the anxiety.

While Rafiki was talking to me, explaining how she felt, she was also working through the emotions. At the same time, I was working with the essential oils to support those emotions that she was experiencing and help her deal with them. She responded with strong interest to rose, angelica root, sandalwood, vetiver, hops, valerian and arnica oil (trauma).

From a dog's point of view, it was difficult to understand why the maid would not be coming back but she gradually began to accept it. I took some time to explain the reason to her, as I also explained the concept of work and why her owners had to leave to go to another place for it. Previously they had worked from home, so the change in this routine had also been upsetting to the dog.

We all agreed that when they left in the morning they would give Rafiki a treat in the form of a nice meaty bone, or a peanut butter filled hoof, or even a toy for her to play with. This would deflect her attention away from the fact that they were leaving. She would still notice they were going but it would not matter as much as she had something else to keep her attention on.

I also mixed up a gel of the oils that she selected. This was to be applied to her chest ten minutes before her owners left to help keep her separation anxiety in check and to reset her current behavior pattern. The gel works on the brain and helps it to relax; she also gets a treat, and thereby we move away from what was once looked upon as a negative pattern towards a positive behavioral change. Rafik's separation anxiety is now a thing of the past. They got into a new routine the very next day and have not looked back since.

How Trauma Leaves the Body

This is Bella, a nine-year-old Labrador with whom I was booked to do a reading. Her owners wanted a general reading—how was she feeling, was she happy with her food, walks, and life in general, and was there anything they could do to make life happier for her? (Awesome owners, eh?) When I scanned her heart area, I picked up a trauma that had happened at the age of 16 months but wasn't worrying her now. She had dealt with it, and it was now right on the edge of the aura, very close to leaving her aura completely.

The early trauma happened when her owners at the time found that having a Labrador was too much to handle and put her up for adoption. She spent a week in a rescue center before being rehomed, but it was enough to make its mark on her heart chakra, as to be expected.

Figure 27: Trauma Progression in a Dog

Figure 27 shows the progression of that trauma, from the heart into the first layer, the physical level, the emotional level, through the mental level, and finally, to the etheric level, before leaving the field completely.

This progression and healing may happen in one lifetime, or it may be carried over through several lifetimes if the issue is not dealt with. For instance, if the dog was rehomed several times in one lifetime and never settled down in another home, the issue might come up again in the next lifetime.

Figure 28: Boss with Spike on Physical Level

CASE STUDY: Boss – Misalignment

Boss was a 9-year-old Pomeranian that I had to do a reading on. In the first ten minutes of the reading he jumped on his father's lap and settled down along his legs, with his head looking at me and his body along his dad's leg (like a hotdog). He then proceeded to show me his energy field, which I have illustrated below. As you can see, there is a spike in his field on the physical level, and it is focused solely in the middle of his body. I wanted to investigate the source of this spike and find out what was going on there, so I did an auric scan by running my hand over the top of his body. I picked up that he had previously hurt his right back leg and hip, when he had jumped off the couch in an odd way. It had not healed the way that it should and was affecting his spine. Boss needed professional help to readjust his hips and spine into alignment, so I suggested to his owners to have a chiropractor assess him.

Sometimes animals are very open when showing their energy field to a healer. Boss was so specific about where his problem was and what he needed that it took only five minutes to discover the source and determine the best way to help him.

I offered him a variety of oils. Boss selected comfrey macerated oil to take orally and a mix of yarrow and wintergreen in a gel to apply externally to support the healing in that leg.

Figure 29: Butch in Full Anger Mode

CASE STUDY: Butch – Anger

Butch is a three-year-old male French bulldog who was neutered about a year before I saw him. He shares his home with his owner and a two-year-old female French bulldog called Sasha. His owner had recently gotten divorced, moved into a new home, and was facing a few tough decisions. She called me in as Butch battled with severe male dominancy and aggression issues. He had been neutered and the owner had tried a pheromone collar to calm him, but neither of these had made a difference. He tried to bite everyone that came into the home without exception, whether family or workmen. The situation has gotten so bad that no one wanted to visit the house anymore as they were terrified of Butch.

I arrived at the house, which was in a complex, and parked my car in front of the garage. I got my kit out of the trunk of the car and walked to the front door. The owner was at the door, which was recessed, with Sasha in her arms to stop her running out; Butch was behind the security gate, barking at me. He hadn't seen me at all; he had just heard the arrival of the car and the trunk closing. The owner asked if she could let him out. Without thinking I said sure. The moment the gate opened and his feet touched the ground, he flew at me, wanting to attack in a very aggressive way, trying to bite me and anything he could find that I had with me.

I immediately used my box to block him, but he still managed to sink his teeth into my sneakers, just missing my toes. The owner came out of the house, flinging her hands in the air, and stated, "You see? That is what he does to everyone who comes here."

I asked her to get control of him and put him inside, which she did by putting him in the garden and behind the sliding glass door. He absolutely detested this, barked and cried, then showed his teeth and unhappiness that I was inside *his* house, in *his* territory, while he was forced to be outside.

While I was speaking to the owner, I pulled the door open a fraction and placed there a few bottles of essential oil that work to calm the mind and male dominancy issues. Butch barked at them angrily, which was fine, as I knew the capillaries in his nose and mouth—the veronasal capillaries—would be taking in the scent of the oil.

The owner admitted that she just could not cope with his behavior anymore as it was ruling her life. She felt that things were getting out of control, which they clearly were. She really loved him but admitted that it was too much for her. She could not walk him anymore, as she felt he wanted to attack all other dogs he encountered, so she only dared walk him every now and then in the evening. She wanted me to explain to him how she felt, which I duly did. There were times when he quietened down and interacted with me telepathically and other times when he was very vocal and upset at what we were discussing. He thought he did his job extremely well and could not understand what all the fuss was about.

The illustration in Figure 29 shows his energetic field in full anger mode. When a dog is aggressive the spikes are red, but when the dog is aggressive or dominant out of protection for himself or his owner the spikes are a silver-metallic color.

One very important point he shared was that he felt he had been taken away from his mother too early. Puppies must be socialized with other dogs before they are six weeks old. If this does not happen, they can become aggressive or frightened of their peers. This was a definite contributing factor. Unfortunately, due to ignorance and not realizing what she was doing, the owner has not helped the situation at all. She was fueling the fire.

Every time someone came to the door, she picked him or his sister up. Maybe in the beginning, it was to stop the dog running out, but because of Butch's bad behavior it had become a reaction to what the owner perceived as a problem, and in Butch's language it had become a threat. Each time she was expecting someone to arrive, she would remind him unintentionally to attack them, as she kept replaying previous incidences in her mind and he was reading and reacting to them. By picking him up, she was saying to him, "I am nervous and worried." By letting him run out the door first, she was telling him that he is the alpha dog in the house and she needed protection ("My mom is nervous of you coming into our home. I am therefore going to react to that and attack whoever it is.").

Mistake number 2 was that she let him run out the door before her, which was allowing his dominancy to come out in full force. She should make him wait and she should go through the door first, in order to reinstate her dominance as the alpha in the house, not him.

When we become anxious or scared, the adrenaline in our body increases, which gives off a scent. Animals pick up this scent and instinctively react to it. In the wild, you would become the prey being hunted; it's how nature works. Butch would smell this fear every time she expected someone and worried that he would attack them.

In this instance, for about three years, this dog had been receiving the wrong kind of messages from the owner.

My suggestions to her were:
- Engage an animal behaviorist who specializes in aggressive cases to help retrain him.
- Sign him up for socialization and behavior classes with a suitably qualified person.
- Become the alpha in the house, not him.
- Change her own behavior in how she greets people at the door.
- Avoid picking him up. Do not think of people visiting as negative.
- Watch her thoughts and what her adrenaline is conveying to him.

The owner did admit that all I suggested was just too overwhelming at the moment and that she was thinking of rehoming him or even putting him to sleep. Sasha was the exact opposite of her brother, loving and kind. She adored and interacted with other dogs and loved being social and missed the outings they used to take because of her brother's behavior. They were now very limited as to what outings they could do because of his aggression. Even the beach was intolerable.

Half an hour into the session, Butch was let back into the house but remained aggressive toward me whenever I moved. The oils had no effect whatsoever (which hardly ever happens, as some are really strong), neither did the talking seem to help; no matter how much love and understanding I sent him, I was being blocked by a razor-sharp etheric field. I am the first to admit that this was the most difficult case I had ever experienced in all the years of doing this job—nothing worked. After two and half hours, I had to concede to myself and the owner that I had tried everything I could think of and left her with the suggestions I had made and some serious thinking to do.

To this day, I still think back and ask myself if I could have done more or something different, and the answer is no, I could not. I would like to save and help everyone and everything, but there are times, such as with Butch, when you need to admit defeat. This was one of those cases, unfortunately.

Interspecies Relationships

Penny, the horse, found herself with a recent addition to her stable: a lovely but scrawny-looking chicken, Buttercup. The two struck up a friendship, with the chicken sleeping in Penny's stable at night. Every evening, Penny would make sure some hay fell to the floor so that her friend could make herself a comfortable bed for the night. The grooms had a tendency to sweep everything in a heap in the mornings and redistribute her bedding, so it became a habit for the chicken to make her nest every night just after supper.

One day, the pair were settling in for the night when Penny accidentally stood on her best friend. A tremendous amount of squawking followed, and Penny was beside herself for hurting her friend. Unfortunately, Buttercup did not survive and had to be put down.

Penny's owner, Tammy, felt bad and assumed that Penny would want another chicken friend from the yard to keep her company. The following evening, she put down a small water bowl and some food, should anyone wish to drop in and keep Penny company. Within an hour, Penny had picked up the water and food bowl and flung them out of her stable. Bewildered, Tammy picked the bowls up and replaced them. Once again, the bowls were flung out of her stable and into her yard. Not wanting to upset her any more than necessary, Tammy called me in for help.

Penny was finding it difficult to forgive herself for stepping on her friend and really missed the scrawny little hen who shared her stable. She felt life was rather unfair and felt cursed with four hooves instead of two feet, as two feet would make her more agile. She requested that her owner refrain from replacing the bowls in her stable, as her heart was broken and she did not want the same thing happening again. RIP, dear little hen.

CASE STUDY: Mousha – Anger

Mousha was a 13-year-old miniature dapple dachshund who had recently been getting up to out-of-character mischief. She had managed to get out of her owner's property twice in the last month, causing much anxiety and concern. This was something she has never done before. Her owner had a horse, so they always went to the livery to visit the horse and then Mousha was allowed to go on a walkabout and explore (within reason).

However, over the last month or two, she had been disappearing for hours on end and no one could find her, resurfacing when she felt like it (again very out of character as she stuck to her owner like a shadow). The last time she did this, she came back looking very stuffed. Being a sausage dog and having a conscientious owner who watched her diet she was quiet trim. Now after her disappearing act, her stomach was bulging and she had obviously been eating some-thing (they did not know what) and had not stopped eating until she was filled to capacity. She had eaten so much, she was also short of breath. Her owner immediately took her to the vet who pumped her stomach and discovered that she had been eating cat food. This happened again the following week, snacking on cat food, but this time she returned not as round. It was a huge yard with four or five different store rooms, but they eventually found the food Mousha was eating.

Needless to say something was up, she was deliberately trying to get out of the yard and looking for food from another source, so I was called in.

Figure 30: Closed-Off Energy Field

Mousha has closed off her energy field towards her owner. Her mental layer is also very enlarged in the front of her body, forcing her will on her owner and establishing dominancy.

Mousha was cross with her owner and had even blocked her energy field to the extent that it felt like she was being shunned by her own animal. Mousha showed me an image of exactly where she went to at the stables—a store room where the cat food was kept—and stated that she was starving, which was why she had recently started seeking out the cat food. She was proud of the fact that she had found herself another source of food, seeing that her owner did not feed her enough!

She complained that of late she always felt hungry and if she could not find food at the stables then she would try and escape from the property and look for it herself in neighboring homes. While she was sharing this information with me, she self-selected rose hydrosol on her chest several times (for anger and trauma). She was only interested in licking large quantities of barleygrass and spirulina, looking for minerals and vitamins that her body was obviously lacking.

Mousha's owner confessed that she had deliberately put her dog on a 24-hour fast on several occasions to try and get her stomach right after her overindulgence of cat food (even after the vet had pumped her stomach). Two months prior to that, someone had commented Mousha could lose a little weight, so her owner had cut back on her food. She was feeding her a raw diet, which is great, but since it had been cut down it was far too little for Mousha, who gets walked every day and receives hydrotherapy once a week. She was always hungry, so she had decided to look for food elsewhere.

Mousha had the opportunity to explain to her owner how she felt and why she was trying to get out of the property and look for food elsewhere. Her owner promised to up her food intake to what it had previously been; in future, to discuss any change in diet and quantity with her vet; and from now on, there would be no more fasting. At the close of the session, both of them were in a much better place energetically and the energy fields had corrected themselves.

Figure 31: Energy Field in Balance Again

Mousha's outer field is now spongelike and not so hard and defensive.
Her heart chakra is open and flowing toward her owner.

2

Chakras

You've probably heard of chakras, or energy vortices, before. This section is for those who haven't, or who don't understand the important, albeit nonphysical, role they play in our system. In fact, to understand chakras, it is important to have a working knowledge of the entire energy field.

In the previous chapter, we discussed the fact that our energy field is a mirror of our physical body, as well as our emotional, mental, and spiritual bodies. Every thought, act, and emotion, both positive and negative, that we experience in our lifetime leaves traces in our aura and also affects our chakras.

Understanding Chakras

The word "chakra" is a Sanskrit word meaning "wheel." Chakras are often referred to as "wheels of light" or "wheels of life" because they appear energetically as spinning wheels or vortices that resemble cones, with both a front and a back side.

Human and animal energy fields have a complex system of chakras. These are formed from our energy field and are vital to the health and wellbeing of all living things. Although universal energy (prana, chi, ki) cannot be seen by the average person, it is all around us and flows in and out of the chakras. These energy vortices, or portals, are located at certain key places throughout the body and are vehicles for receiving, assimilating, and expressing this life force energy.

As an analogy, think of a car that has an air filter to clean all the air that flows through the engine. In the human body, we have lungs to filter the air we breathe. In our energy fields, we have spinning vortices that look a little like round car air filters, only they allow universal energy to flow two ways, both inward and outward.

The chakra system can also be likened to a "map of consciousness" for each individual person and animal. The chakras vary in brightness, depth, size, and openness, depending on the health and vitality of the being they belong to. As you can see in Figure 32, each chakra governs an area of the body, including specific glands and organs in the physical body, as well as emotional, mental, and spiritual aspects of consciousness.

Although there may be some variation, human chakras are generally associated with a standard color:

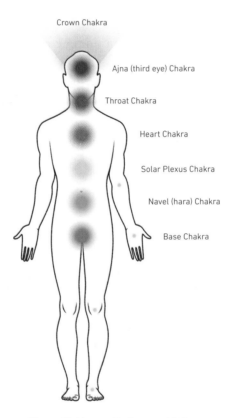

Figure 32: Human Chakras and Colors

The Major Horse Chakras

Just as in a human, a horse's chakras, and the meridians that connect them, lie within the horse's energy field. Life force energy is filtered via the chakras into this energy field, and from there it flows into the meridians. Meridians are like invisible, energetic veins that run through the body and transport energy around it. This energy affects the various glands of the endocrine system, which eventually impacts the horse on a physical level.

Figure 33: Horse Chakras

Color	Chakra	Location
	Crown	Top of the Head
	Third Eye	Above the Eyes
	Throat	Throat
	Heart	Heart
	Seat of the Soul	Mid-Heart
	Solar Plexus	Stomach
	Sacral	Sex Organs
	Base	Above the Tail

Whereas humans have seven major chakras (although an eighth chakra, called the "higher heart," can sometimes be seen developing), all horses have eight. We named the eighth chakra the Seat of the Soul. Afterwards, in researching this book, we found that others had also confirmed its existence and named it the brachial chakra. This unique chakra is located between the shoulders, below the neck and above the scapula.

The degree to which a horse's chakra system is healthy and balanced plays a large role in how this life force energy vitalizes him. When tuning into a horse's energy system, it's possible to pick up if the chakras are looking and functioning as they should.

From this, we can also get an idea of the untold stories of their past and present, and then do whatever we can, to the best of our knowledge and ability, to help get everything back into balance and in optimal working order again.

Root Chakra (or Base Chakra) – Red

This chakra is situated at the end of the spine, at the base of the tail. It is related to physical world issues, including grounding, survival instinct, pecking order, security, trust, courage, and patience.

Sacral Chakra – Orange

This chakra is located just above the base of the spine, and goes all the way through to the genitals. It manages all aspects of procreation, including the sexual organs, as well as assimilation of food, physical life force, and vitality.

Solar Plexus Chakra – Yellow

This chakra is found above the hips or pelvis and relates to personal power and will. This is the key center for the sympathetic nervous system, digestive system, metabolism, and emotions.

Heart Chakra – Green (or Pink)

This chakra is situated in the heart area, extending through from the bottom of the mane to the mid-chest area, governing divine and unconditional love and the human/animal bond. It also energizes the blood and physical body with life force.

Throat Chakra – Sky Blue

This is situated in the throat area, including both the front and back of the neck around the mane. It manages all aspects of communication and creative expression, especially conscious communication with intent. It also relates to truth, knowledge, and wisdom.

Third Eye Chakra (or Brow Chakra) – Indigo

This can be found on the forehead between the eyes and is highly developed in most horses. It is about psychic insight and telepathy, which is the way horses communicate. It is also linked to concentration and soul realization.

Crown Chakra – White (or Violet)

This chakra is situated on top of the head, between the ears. It relates to connection with life force and with the divine (God/Goddess, Universe, Spirit), as well as divine wisdom, understanding, selfless service, and perception beyond space and time.

Seat of the Soul (Eighth Chakra)

The Seat of the Soul is located within the chest, just in front of the heart, and is the center for horse-human connection, bonding, and healing. It is the ultimate center of divine love and is the core of the energetic system, holding and recording the soul's intent for this lifetime. This chakra appears to be bigger than the rest, and is bi-directional as it extends to the front and rear of the body, as well as above and below, just like a star. On certain horses, the eighth chakra is very evident when working with them; however, others are reluctant to give of themselves. It begins to expand when a new level of spiritual awareness is initiated, and also helps to support and expand the energy of the heart chakra.

Seeing or Sensing a Chakra

Healthy auras and chakras are moving energy, they contract and expand in relation to the environment they are in. As they are multi-dimensional, you cannot just place your hands in an area that you know has a chakra and feel the outline of it – it simply doesn't work that way. If you were to run your hands over a horse's body, hoping to see or feel it, you might at first think there is nothing there, until you suddenly get a sensation that feels a bit like candyfloss.

Figure 34: What a Chakra Feels Like

The Changing Nature of Chakras

In the table below, I have documented what the chakra looks like if you were looking at it with the naked eye and how it changes in everyday life for various reasons.

Animal Chakra	What it Means
	A normal, healthy animal chakra looks like this. It is three-dimensional and constantly expanding and contracting.

Animal Chakra	What it Means
	If some kind of trauma happened or happens, you may see spots in and around the chakra, which indicate negative belief systems and physical or emotional pain. The spots are often debris related to trauma: physical, mental, or emotional. The spots might also indicate that the horse has taken on the trauma of another person or animal. There are two ways in which the spots can change: Either they become more tangible and solid because the issue gets re-triggered (see illustrations below and on the next page). Or, with the right support or changes in beliefs, the issue is released and the spots get dispersed. If the emotion or trauma is dealt with, the spots leave the area in a swirl and disappear. The amount of density of the cloud indicates the level the issue is sitting at, i.e. the more spots the more active and the closer to becoming solid the trauma is, thus becoming the only truth in the consciousness. The less spots the closer the trauma is to being resolved and released.
	If the energy of the trauma is contained and crystallizes, moving so deeply into the consciousness of the horse that it becomes part of them, the spots become solid. This also happens when there is an activation of an issue, like an emotional incident. When a trauma becomes activated, it starts to beam out and the energy becomes more solid. Whatever is experienced in this area of the body is intense. When you are able to sense it, it likely has more solid boundaries.

Animal Chakra	What it Means
	This image shows a chakra that is activating.
	If there is a swirl over a chakra, with a move to the side, it indicates that the horse is actively communicating and engaging with others.
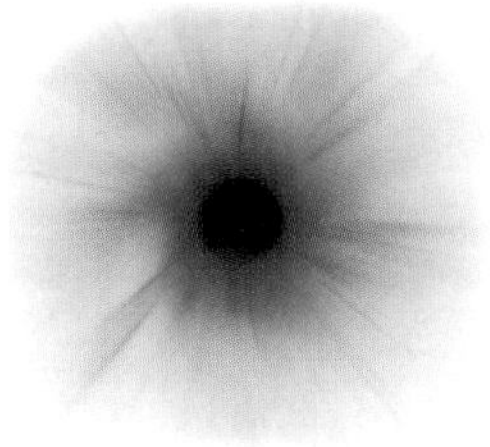	When the animal feels an emotion, such as love, this radiates outwards in the shape of rays.

Figure 35: The Changing Nature of Chakras

3

Color

Color is all around us, in every shape and form. Our auras are filled with color. It helps to define our daily existence and add value and meaning to our lives, mostly without us even being aware of it. Have you ever put on an item of clothing, only to look in the mirror and immediately take it off again as you just didn't feel like wearing that color that day?

All energy of whatever quality is continually vibrating, and an object or energy field assumes the color, shade, or tint belonging to that specific rate of vibration. Every color has a distinct energy frequency and vibration linked to its wavelength.

In Barbara Ann Brennan's book *Hands of Light*, she explains that scientists have analyzed color wave patterns using an electronic measuring device. The frequency bands (Hz = Hertz or cycles per second) were registered as follows:

Color	Frequency
Blue	250 – 275 Hz
Green	250 - 475 Hz
Yellow	500 – 700 Hz
Orange	950 – 1050 Hz
Red	1000 – 1200 Hz
Violet	1000 – 2000 Hz
White	1100 – 2000 Hz

Figure 36: Frequency Bands of Color

Color as Perceived by Animals

Many people seem to believe that animals cannot see color. However, if an animal has cones in their eyes, they will be able to see some color. Their eyesight may be stronger or weaker than ours, depending on the animal. Scientists have established that animals rely on their sight and senses to find food. They can distinguish between red and blue berries, for example, and whether a fruit is ripe or not. Animals also identify predators, using not only shape and smell but also color.

Every animal I have ever worked with has been able to see color and identify it. Although they might not see it in exactly the same way the human eye perceives it, they can put a color in my mind and talk about it. When a competitive horse tells his owner that he really does not like the color yellow, you know he is very determined to win. The third place rosette is yellow, so anything yellow to him means third place, rather than the first place he wants.

Another less competitive and more laid back horse, who is ridden for enjoyment and pleasure, may love the color yellow, as to them it is all about happiness and flowers, and therefore positive.

It's interesting to note that nearly every animal has a favorite color they enjoy and find comfort in, and they often bring it up in a reading.

Reading Colors in an Animal

As we live in the physical, we perceive colors as being physical and often do not realize that they have a psychic counterpart. When doing readings, or working with animals, it is normal to pick up different colors in their energy fields.

The majority of people cannot actually see color with their naked eye, though. Instead, you may simply sense, or become aware of, a specific color in a certain area, which is related to the vibration of that area of the body. I usually see colors clairvoyantly or feel them on a high-sense perception level. All too often, though, people pick up a certain color or image, and then try to figure out what it means by linking it to the closest chakra. It doesn't necessarily work like that, as sometimes a color is not related to the chakra at all. Rather, it is related to a physical or emotional condition that is being experienced and reflected in the aura, more often than not in the emotional level.

When Melana and I first started researching this book, that everything in the aura, including the changes that happen during a session, is defined by color. Energy vibrations change in response to a change in condition or emotion, and it was these changes in the field, and the way the energy moved and flowed, that told us exactly what was going on.

When I scan the energy field of an animal by holding my hands just above their body, I try to quiet my mind and just be in the moment, without any preconceived ideas or worries that I might not pick anything up. As I move my hands carefully around the body, feeling the field, sometimes I first pick up hot or cold areas.

Cold generally indicates a blocked chakra on the emotional level, which needs energetic healing, and this also guides me on what oils to offer the animal to help this process. Hot indicates inflammation in the physical layer of the aura. If there are past injuries in the body, and they want me to be aware of them, I pick it up on the mental level. If they don't want me to see an old hurt, though, they simply block it off so I can't see it.

As I continue the scan, I become aware of a specific color or colors in the energy field. Sometimes there is no sensation of hot or cold at all, and it's simply the color I pick up that tells me something is wrong.

From my own personal experience, I now know what emotional, mental, or physical issues the different colors indicate:

Color	Auric Level	Emotion
Red	Emotional and mental level Physical level	Anger, frustration; still tender injury or other trauma
Orange	Physical level: Inflammation	An awareness of discomfort in the physical body
Pink	Emotional level	Love and positive emotions; connectedness
Yellow	Mental and emotional level Physical level: Damaged ligaments or cartilage Bile - liver	Release of old beliefs or activation of the mental consciousness. Emotion would depend on whether past or present tense and how it affected them
Green	Emotional level Physical level	Healing and release of emotion held in this area, i.e. separation, anxiety. Healing and release of pain
Blue	Physical level	Discomfort, nerve damage

Color	Auric Level	Emotion
Brown	Emotional, mental and physical levels	A tender or bruised area; stagnation (energy not moving and flowing) Needs to be activated – check chakras
Purple	Mental area and slightly above usually over the back Purple is not a common color, and is only seen in more evolved animals where the third eye has been opened, in which case you feel that connection as a wow moment and will never forget it	Spiritual or past life issue; higher consciousness; connected to their Purpose
Black	Mental and emotional level	Blocked energy; crystallized beliefs around pain and trauma
Silver or Grey	Mental level: Stagnation	It feels dull – there is no emotion just a dead area

Figure 37: Correlation of Colors, Auric Levels, and Emotion

Here is an example of what a horse looks like to someone who can see or feel energy. Not everything will be seen at once. What you are seeing is the accumulation of findings when doing a reading:

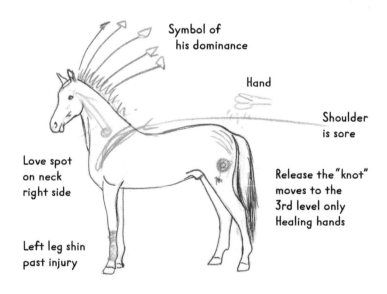

Figure 38: High-Sense Perception of a Horse

Thermal Imaging

Thermal imaging cameras also use color to depict an inflammation or injury in an animal. These are thermal images of a horse that was having issues with his feet. A thermal imaging camera can be used as a diagnostic tool to identify problem areas in bones and soft tissues. It can help diagnose inflammation or injury, and it can also monitor the recovery progress. A camera pointed at different areas in the body reveals temperature differences. Through this, possible problems can be detected up to three weeks before the animal starts showing physical signs of something being wrong.

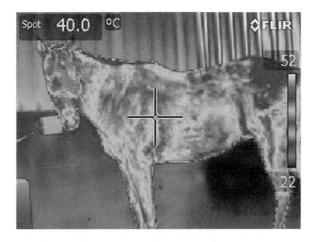

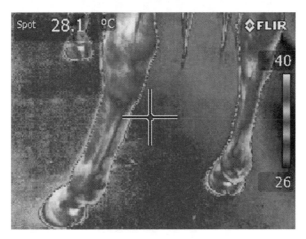

Figure 39: Thermal Imaging for Diagnosis

4

Changes in the
Energy Fields

In the previous chapters, we looked at auras and chakras to start to understand their role in the energy field, along with some symbols that indicate something going on. Because energy is flowing and changing all the time, the next step is to understand what happens in the energy field when humans and horses actively engage with each other and/or communicate.

When they become domesticated, horses, dogs and cats seem to be able to change their field in order to interact with humans and make it easier for us. It's as if they tune their frequency to a bandwidth that we can better understand and connect with.

Have you ever experienced trying to explain a concept to someone but they just can't seem to get it? In essence, you are just not "on the same wave length." Sometimes though, you can slightly alter what you're saying, and how you are saying it, to help the other person understand. It's a bit like turning on your car radio. The signal may be fuzzy and a horrible noise comes out, so you twist the dial or press a button, searching through the stations until you find one you're comfortable with. Essentially, that's exactly what animals are doing for us when they adapt to our wavelengths.

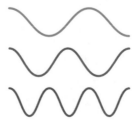

Figure 40: Wavelengths

Conversely, when working with wild animals, you might need to tune into a different frequency to get the same level of information you are getting with domesticated animals. A wild animal's frequency is no less developed than that of a domesticated animal's, it's just different and they tend not to adapt their wavelength so easily to ours.

The Communication Process

This is a step-by-step, mutual process. For each step, we will look at the animal first, then the human. We have just used the figure of a horse as an example. In a communication session it seems that three energy phases take place:

1. Initial connection
2. Active communication with sending and receiving
3. Activation of healing, whether consciously or not (by both parties)

First Phase:
Initial Connection – Animals

Figure 41: First Phase – Initial Activation for the Animal

Activation Centers of Animal's Initial Connection

1. They feel a pressure in their heart area.
2. They actively make a decision about whether or not to communicate (in cats, it's ego-based).
3. They accept you as worthy of communication (or not).
4. The throat chakra opens at the front and back (green – Fig 41). (Cats make the conscious decision to connect from the heart of the mind.)
5. The crown chakra is activated and connects with universal energy (yellow – Fig 41).

STEP 1 They feel a pressure in their heart area

To begin the process, the animal communicator mentally visualizes their own heart opening, and then sees a stream of light leaving their heart and reaching out to the animal's heart. Both the animal and the human can experience a slight pressure in the heart area at this stage. The animal first feels the connection in the Seat of the Soul.

STEP 2 They actively make a decision about whether or not to communicate

During this process, the animal evaluates whether you are worthy of communication. If they're not happy with you, they can close down again. If you continue reaching out, meaning you just persist in trying to connect in a loving and calm way they can re-evaluate you and possibly change their minds until they are hopefully happy with you and there is a firm connection established.

STEP 3 They accept you as worthy of communication (or not)

If you get this far, they actively open the front of their heart chakra, which allows them to receive the love energy connection. The Seat of the Soul is then activated.

Although this chakra spins all the time, when it is activated, it is as if it lights up. Imagine a gentle, flowing stream, with a beam of sunlight shining on a certain area of the water. That area seems to come to life, sparkling so it stands out from the rest of the stream around it – it can be captivating. This is what the Seat of the Soul looks like when that chakra is activated.

STEP 4 The throat chakra opens at the front and back

Next, the back of the throat chakra is stimulated and also activates, opening up the communication process. At this stage, they will normally want to know who you are and why you are there. If they have not heard their owner talking about a healer or an animal communicator coming to talk to them, it can be a bit of a shock that a human being can hear them.

Their reaction varies hugely from animal to animal. Some will stand in front of you, giving you the eye and feeling your energy, like a detective, to find out if you are who you claim to be. Others are just plain curious. Often, when you explain you want to help them and to build the bond between them and their owner, they are only too happy to have you there.

There have been times where they have blocked me from connecting. In those cases, I then work with the oils first. Once they start feeling the benefits of the plant extracts, they realize my intention is only good and they then relax into the session.

They will only let you see their emotional body once they have established their place and dominance with you. There has to be trust before they will allow you to scan them and pick up any information.

STEP 5 The crown chakra is activated and connects with universal energy

A yellow stream of energy extends out of the crown chakra into the cosmos, as the mind is activated, and the horse connects to universal energy.

First Phase:
Initial Connection – Humans

Nearly all animal communicators will tell you that when connecting to any animal, they do so through the heart chakra. I mentally visualize my heart opening, and then build a connection, or bridge of love, from my heart to the animal's heart.

For this connection to take place, the animal communicator needs to be working with unconditional love. They also need a clear mind, with no preconceived thoughts or ideas of the information they will be getting. This very natural process occurs in everyday life with our own animals, especially when we are comfortable and at ease around them.

It seems obvious that when opening your heart chakra and trying to connect with an animal, that would be happening in your energy field.

What was surprising was just how many other things actually happen in your energy field at the same time.

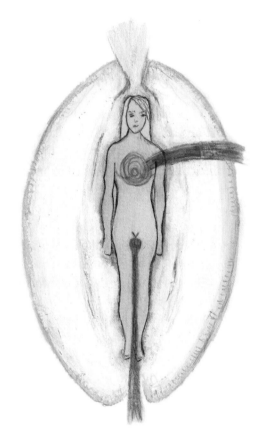

Figure 42: First Phase – Initial Connection for the Human

Activation Centers of Human's Initial Connection
1. Back of the heart chakra opens.
2. Base chakra is activated and energy moves up to the sacral chakra.
3. Front of the heart chakra activates and energy leaves the Animal. Communicator's heart and flows to the animal.
4. Throat chakra activates for communication.
5. Crown chakra activates and a yellow stream of energy. connects to universal energy.

STEP 1   The back of the heart chakra opens

Some chakras in the human body have both a front and a back side. The first thing that happens during this connection is that the back of the heart chakra opens - not the front, as is commonly thought.

STEP 2   The base chakra is activated

Energy begins to move up from the earth, through both feet and legs, and up through the base chakra, regardless of whether you have consciously grounded yourself before the session or not. Although the base chakra is always working, as the energy enters it, it is activated more fully by the extra influx of energy. The base chakra is commonly seen by mystics and psychics as red, yet the energy that moves up from the ground and enters this chakra is purple.

STEP 3   The front heart chakra opens and is activated

The next thing to happen is a swirling motion of pink energy around the front of the heart chakra. This is the conscious activation of the connection, or the bridge of love. Pink energy then flows from the heart area to the animal. Once the heart chakra is open, then the consciousness of the animal communicator starts moving toward the animal. If the animal is receptive to this invitation to connect, then his consciousness meets that of the animal communicator.

STEP 4   The throat chakra opens

As the throat chakra opens, it is activated by purple swirling energy for active communication.

STEP 5   The crown chakra activates

Finally, in the initial connection phase, a yellow stream of energy extends out of the crown chakra and connects to universal energy.

Due to the energetic interchange taking place while the initial connection is happening, there will already be information about each other being shared between the animal communicator and the horse.

Think back to when you were a child visiting the beach. You would take your little fishing net and bucket and head off to the rocks. You might first use your net to scoop everything you could from the rock pools into your bucket. Then you might put your hand into the water and try and touch anything left, feeling the roughness of the sea urchins, the slipperiness of seaweed. You might even notice the grainy feel of the sand squeezing between your toes. The same kind of thing happens in the initial connection with an animal, only on a telepathic level. You are connecting energetically and feeling each other out.

Because of this, even at this point you may be aware of information already coming through. You will be able to pick up each other's moods, for example—happy, sad, boisterous, calm, content, angry, and so on. You will also be able to determine the level of evolution or consciousness of the horse and get a feel for their personality—whether they are the sensitive or competitive, proud type. If the animal communicator is nervous, the horse will sense that nervousness. Usually they are inquisitive about what is happening, as they have felt the subtle, energetic changes.

Second Phase: Active Communication

In this stage, both the animal and the person are actively involved in a dialogue with each other, both of them sending and receiving information. This isn't necessarily the same kind of conversation two people would have, as it takes place using thought forms. Most animal communicators receive images and emotions around that image, and it is then up to them to try and interpret the information, understand what they are receiving and then pass that information to the owner.

To give you an example, I was once shown an image of a field with lots of colorful tents, the smell of pancakes in the air, crowds of people walking around, and loud music being played through speakers, which came with a sense of curiosity and intuitiveness. I interpreted this as a festival. The horse loved it all, as so much was happening in a usually quiet paddock. He enjoyed the colors, the smells, and the people. His owner was able to confirm the event, and said that he had stood and watched it the entire morning, enjoying every minute. Some animals would have hated having loud humans disrupting their day, but he loved it so much that he brought it up in the reading and wanted to know when it would be happening again.

Working with owners who are open-minded is such a pleasure. It can be very difficult doing a reading where they keep silent throughout to "test" whether you are really connecting to their animal. They would gain so much more by interacting with the animal communicator and with their animal. Animals want and appreciate confirmation of life events and of their likes and dislikes.

Sometimes owners are worried about what you might find out, which could be as simple as the fact that the horse loved the smell of the cream soda the kids had while they were picnicking in the field. I don't judge what I pick up; I simply pass on the message. It's often those little details that make a reading so special and can cause either laughter or tears.

I just love how much information they share about their likes, dislikes, and general well-being. It truly shifts the bond between owner and animal, enriching it and creating a more loving and fulfilling relationship.

So let's look at what happens for both the horse and the human during this dialogue.

Figure 43: Second Phase – Active Communication between Horse and Human

Active Communication

1. Cloud forms between the human and the horse.
2. Thought forms are sent from the back of the horse's throat chakra.
3. Emotions are sent from horse's back solar plexus.
4. Universal energy extends from the animal communicator's head.
5. Animal communicator's crown and third eye chakra remain open.
6. Information is transferred.

STEP 1 A cloud forms between the human and the animal

This is where the images and information are sent and stored. It's a bit like sending a message from your mobile phone. That message sits somewhere on the system (in "the cloud") until it is opened and read by the receiver. Often animals are frustrated as they are continually trying to connect and communicate with us. Their message stays in the cloud, however, if we are not (yet) open to receiving it.

STEP 2 Thought forms are sent from the horse's throat chakra

Thought forms leave the animal's energy field from the throat chakra at the back of the neck. It happens from the unconscious level (Figure 43), and it seems the back of the chakras in both the animal's and human's energy fields are more dominant than the front when connecting.

STEP 3 Emotions are sent from the horse's solar plexus chakra

Remember that the solar plexus is the center of personal power and will. It is also the key center for physical communication with humans, as well as managing the sympathetic nervous system, digestive system, metabolism, and emotions. During the communication phase, the back of the horse's solar plexus chakra is activated, and a lovely light blue energy leaves the chakra and enters the cloud bank. This is the emotional part of what they are trying to convey to us, which can encompass the full spectrum of emotions: happiness, sadness, grief, devastation, longing for a friend or past owner, emotional hurt, and so on.

STEP 4 Energy extends from the animal communicator's head

In the animal communicator's energy field, energy can be seen leaving the head, usually from the brow area, extending upward and outward, around the entire circumference of the head.

STEP 5 The animal communicator's crown chakra remains open

The yellow energy connecting the animal communicator to universal energy is still very much present, and it allows information to also come through from a different source than the animal. Although the images here document what happens in my energy field when in session with animals, we are also all connected and guided by a higher power.

In some people, this yellow energy will be more prevalent and brighter, as the more you use your intuition and try to connect, the stronger the color and the higher the energy will rise. For those who are still learning, it might be smaller and not as bright. Tapping into or using energy is a little like going to the gym: the more you use the muscle, the stronger it grows.

STEP 6 Information is transferred

The energy the animal has sent leaves the cloud and enters the human's crown chakra. It then moves through the human's energetic system to the brain, where it is received, interpreted and then verbally conveyed to the owner. At this stage, the throat and heart chakras are also still active.

Going in the other direction, when the animal communicator asks a question, it leaves their crown chakra and enters the cloud, from where it is then transferred to the animal.

What is really interesting is that the color that leaves the chakra is not the same color as the chakra from which it flows. For example, yellow energy leaves the crown chakra, which is usually described as violet.

After the session, the energy fields of both the animal communicator and the animal gradually return to normal.

Figure 44: Second Phase – Human Response

CASE STUDY: Burning Bright

Have you ever experienced something deeply, yet not been able to express it in words? The same thing happens to animals, and instead, they sometimes try to express those emotions through the animal communicator's body.

In the case of Burning Bright, a seven-year-old gelding, I constantly had to clear my throat while I was working with him. I was battling to find the right words to adequately explain things to his owner and rider, and I was feeling the emotions but had difficulty voicing them, indicating a blocked throat chakra. This was his way of telling the owners that he could not always say what needed to be said. Once we figured this out and spoke about it, he then began readily interacting in the session.

Burning Bright

Then whenever I said something he did not like (sometimes he felt I revealed too much information), he would stamp his front foot. He was telling his owners that this was the way he showed them what he liked and did not like, both on a physical and emotional level. He also used it to show when he did not like someone or did not approve of what was being spoken about. When he brought this to his owner's attention, it helped to develop a much deeper relationship and level of understanding between them.

In fact, this is one of the easiest things to do if you want information from your horse. Just ask a yes/no question, and notice if they stomp their feet, or nod their head for a yes and shake it for a no.

An additional note here: I revisited Burning Bright a year later at a different stable yard. The new yard was not a competitive one, and was therefore much more relaxed and easy-going. What a turnaround! He is still winning all his events, but is much more happy and relaxed. He didn't stomp his foot once in the session with me, and I didn't have to clear my throat at all. He just loved telling me about the great new yard and how happy he was. It was lovely to see—my case notes were nearly nonexistent!

Third Phase: Healing

Healing Hands

When connecting to an animal with utmost respect and love, we exchange energy. Love energy is the highest frequency there is, and it is unconditional and pure. With no expectations, it is complete acceptance of another. Horses also have different levels of consciousness: when you send an animal healing, it can enter on one level and then move to another.

Sometimes, when you want to help an animal, all that is needed is to stand with your hands open and mentally send out loving and healing energy. They recognize this and usually move closer to you to allow better placement of your hands.

Frequency Shifts

What I am about to describe has happened to me often, and at first, I thought I was doing something wrong when tuning into the color I needed to use.

Although I know all the colors and how they energetically affect the body during healing, when I'm in session, I don't actively make a choice based on that knowledge. Instead, I find myself intuitively sending healing to wherever in the body I feel it is needed. I simply hold my hands over the area and let intuition and a higher power take charge of guiding the energy flow. Because I like to understand the why's and how's of energy healing, only afterwards do I sometimes wonder why a specific color was used, especially if it doesn't make sense to me.

For example, I have held my hands over an area that is inflamed and seen my hands as orange, which indicates they are specifically charged with orange energy. In several cases, Melana picked up the inflammation, and also saw my hands as orange, but the horse changed the color to indigo blue, then light blue. Only then did the energy enter the horse's body. I couldn't understand why my hands didn't just charge with blue, then send that, as it was obviously the color that was needed by the animals.

Several years later, I finally understood what was happening. The color orange is measured at 950 Hz, so it is about charging the field; in this case, my hands. Inflammation in the body always gives off heat, which needs to be cooled down (think about how we rush to the freezer for a packet of frozen peas when we need to treat injuries and/or stop swelling). The energy that is needed to cool and calm inflammation is blue. It's a subtler frequency, with indigo at 400 Hz and light blue at around 250/300 Hz. If I had sent orange healing energy, I would have done a lot more harm than good in the inflamed area.

Figure 45: Energy Flow of Healing Hands – Side View

This is what it looks like when the hands give off energy – the energy is flowing down then –, or when you are feeling an animal's energy.

At times, it has been obvious that animals can be actively involved in healing but to what extent has never really been documented. There are hundreds of stories about how animals have helped heal humans, and vice versa. But I would never have known had I not seen it for myself that animals have the capacity to alter and change the frequency of the healing they receive. They are even more remarkable than we realize.

Figure 46: Energy Flow of Healing Hands from Above

CASE STUDY: Frequency Change

This horse was experiencing stiffness in the area from the dock to the rump, which he wanted relieved. The pattern shows the stiffness and the way the horse wanted the healing. In similar cases, I have sent green healing from the front dock to the rear rump. However, in this instance he wanted me to send the healing from the rump to the dock (shoulder), the reverse of the usual way. When doing the healing I used the color green; however, he decided he wanted a different, more energizing color and changed it from green to orange.

Looking at the frequencies again, green is commonly used in energy healing as it's a good gentle healer. It was intended to release tensed-up processes; in this case, muscles. By changing the healing frequency to orange, and moving the energy up his back and into his shoulder, it warmed and stimulated a wider area. He needed this bigger area of his body charged and raised the frequency of the energy to do just that.

I have noticed that if I send the healing in a reverse motion from stomach toward the rear, the horse will release wind several times, if dealing with stomach issues. If this happens, I carry on sending the energy until no more wind is released.

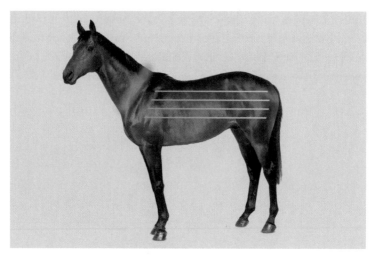

Figure 47: Energy Flow from Rump to Neck

Letting Go and Letting God

As humans we sometimes try to control our lives and the situations around us, and this is not always in our best interests. When we surrender to a higher power, put our logical minds aside, and allow ourselves to open up to an intuitively guided level of healing, we often find that the energy we are channeling is not only beneficial to us but also to everyone round us, both human and animal. The saying "Let go and let God" applies here; doing so moves us all to a higher level of consciousness.

An Experiment

When communicating with animals, I always experience a tangible shift in my own energy levels. There are times when the effects of doing a reading take their toll, especially after a hectic day, leaving me physically and psychologically exhausted.

Sometimes, it feels as if my body experiences a power surge when I connect. I also often experience the emotions of the animal, as well as some of the physical conditions, such as how a saddle feels on my back or the bit feels in my mouth. As a result, I began to wonder if doing a reading has a physical or energetic effect on the human body.

A Scio™ (Scientific Conscious Interface Operational System) machine is an electrophysiological biofeedback system. Many holistic practitioners and naturopaths use it to get information about what is happening inside the body. Electrodes are placed around your head, ankles, and wrists, then electrical impulses are sent from the Scio machine through your body. The body is an electrical field, made up of positive and negative charges, and responds to electrical impulses. Any resistance encountered or stressors created is measured with a Scio machine in volts, amps, and oscillations. The device measures 16 standard electrical parameters in your body and also checks your subconscious mind.

I was curious to see if my energy changed at all during a session and if a machine could pick it up. A Scio reading was done upfront and then again during a session in which I was working telepathically with a dog.

These are the indicators the person operating the machine looks for:

80 –100 = Healthy reaction
Above 100 = Stress exhaustion

Indicators	First calibration reading	In session reading an animal	Notes
Environmental lifestyle stresses	126	128	My environmental stress went up slightly. I was stressed doing something like this
Physical ability to continue current lifestyle	116	105	My ability to function better improved as stress exhaustion reduced
Mental stresses	121	107	Mental stress went down
Lifestyle balance: work/home/social	114	127	Went up
Energetic self image	112	128	Went up
Adrenal function – the ability to maintain current stressors	57	64	Improved
Serotonin levels – natural self satisfaction	25	49	Improved quite dramatically
Resistance – ease of energy flow through the body	80	80	Stayed the same

Indicators	First calibration reading	In session reading an animal	Notes
Hydration – ease of fluid flow through the body	72	81	Improved
Oxidative stress – rate at which the body is oxidizing (influences aging and susceptibility to disease)	64	59	Improved
pH: acid/alkalinity reaction (65 – 70 ideal)	67	67	Stayed the same
Cellular vitality (10 is excellent; 6 is normal)	4	3	Went down

Figure 48: Example of Biofeedback through a Scio Machine

Emotions that showed significantly high readings at the first calibration:

Aggression: 236

Once in session:

My emotive state: 151
Satisfaction: 141
Inadequacy: 136

IN SUMMARY: Doing a reading is stressful, and that shows up in the body. I totally understand this, as the reader wants to bring accurate information through for their client and their animal.

Emotionally, I functioned better as my serotonin went up. The lifestyle balance was thrown out, though (I was in work mode, so I'm not surprised by that).

Note: At the time of the reading, I was going through a divorce, having boundary issues with my teenagers, in the process of building a business while keeping my head above water, writing this book, and extremely stressed and not leading a balanced lifestyle, so many of the results above weren't surprising.

5

Essential Oils & Zoopharmacognosy

I use both animal communication and a practice called zoopharmacognosy when working with an animal. The latter gives domesticated animals the opportunity to self-select medicinal plant extracts, such as algae, clays, essential oils, and macerates. When I first heard of this, I felt like I'd found what I'd been searching for my entire life. While some people never realize their purpose in life, I am lucky enough to have found mine and to be able to combine two things that I love so successfully.

In this chapter, I will be discussing specific oils and how Melana and I have seen them work for an animal on an energetic level, both emotionally and physically. What follows is a brief outline of the essential oils and extracts used in a typical session, which constitute part of my work and will help in your understanding of this aspect.

Although each case is different, when starting a session, I sometimes choose a range of essential oils to work with before doing the reading based on what I pick up when first meeting the animal. The reason for this is purely psychological and comes from a place of respect and knowing. I first build trust and rapport with the animal by offering it healing oils, before connecting on a communication level, if I feel that it is needed.

However, there have been times when I have arrived to do a session and found that there is a physical condition such as inflammation, pain, or colic. The animal intuitively knows that there is something in my kit to help and wants to explore everything I have inside immediately. In that case, I would choose to offer extracts first, as I know they will help, and later on, when the animal is more comfortable, connect and do a reading.

On other occasions, the animal knows the minute I walk into the paddock, or put my kit down on the kitchen floor, that everything in it is for them and they are prepared to wait. They want to talk first, and that is what we do. They guide the session.

I never try to read an animal when working with the oils, as some of the oils work on the limbic (emotional) area of the brain. Just like ours, an animal's mind is a magnificent hard drive full of memories of what they have experienced in their life, along with the accompanying emotions, such as happiness, contentment, anger, fear, insecurity, and jealousy. Some of these may be shared in the communication session a little later on, and some simply need to be experienced, worked through, or released.

Essential Oil Distillation – Distilling Roman Chamomile

Far too many animals are separated or weaned from their mothers too young. Even if they aren't too young, just the experience of being separated from a mother is tough. Being shouted at as a pup or a foal, poked and prodded by a vet, or moved to another place is extremely traumatic for every animal, irrespective of the type of fur or skin they have.

It's for this reason that I generally start with the oils and plant extracts, so emotional trauma can be cleared. Also, it can be very disconcerting trying to focus on connecting to an animal when all they want to do is stare at the box of extracts. So I let them guide the session. By the time we have finished with the oils, they are happier, more relaxed, and feeling comfortable enough to open up to me and their owner, and I can then move on to doing an auric scan.

Important – Please Note!

To work with animals in this way, you need to be trained in zoopharmacognosy and have herbal pharmacology knowledge. I have studied at great length and have experience gathered over a vast number of sessions, so I know how to work with animals and essential oils and what behavioral and physical responses to watch out for. Unless you have a similar background and skills, please do not rush out to buy these oils and try them on your own animals. If handled and used incorrectly, they can be dangerous or even fatal.

What Are Essential Oils?

Essential oils are extracted from the seeds, leaves, bark, roots, and flowers of different plants. The extraction process is done in different ways, depending on the plant. Different plant extracts are used in zoopharmacognosy; essential oils are just one category.

Many plants have minute fat-soluble constituents stored in tiny sacs, and the oils derived from them are volatile. Steam distillation of the plants forces the sacs of oil to burst, and the result is essential oil. Secondary metabolites are present in the oils and have medicinal properties. When a plant is stressed, its concentration of oils increases as a survival mechanism, and this is when the plants are harvested and distilled. Growers therefore deliberately stress plants to increase the yield in certain plants, such as lavender, rosemary, and buchu. In South Africa, the growing of plants for the purposes of distillation has steadily increased over the last few years, making certain oils more accessible to the market.

Aromatics or Hydrosols

The steam that is collected in the process of essential oil distillation becomes the hydrosol (also referred to as aromatic water) that we also use in sessions. They contain elements of the essential oil.

Absolutes

These are concentrated, aromatic, oily mixtures extracted from plants using solvent extraction techniques. An absolute essential oil like rose or violet leaf is generally solvent-extracted instead of steam-distilled.

Not all plants have sacs that can release oils, (e.g., the South African healing legume cancer bush, Sutherlandia frutescens), so those plants need to be ingested and are offered to the animal as a dried herb. An essential oil cannot be made from every plant in nature. The steam distillation process can alter the chemical properties of the plant, and therefore, of the oil. For example, German chamomile should be a deep, dark blue due to the presence of chamazulene, an anti-inflammatory substance in the plant. Because the chamazulene in the oil is activated (due to the heat) when it is steam-distilled, its properties are more concentrated than they are in the dried plant and you have a much higher concentration of chamazulene.

Macerated Oil

We also use infused or macerated oils, which is plant material that is soaked in a base oil. This is done to obtain their aroma or for the healing properties of the plant to pass through to the oil. For example, a plant that is commonly used in zoopharmacognosy is St. John's wort. Hypericum is a constituent (property) of St. John's wort and cannot survive outside the plant unless it is in macerated oil.

Types of Oils

There are several grades of essential oils:
- Therapeutic grade oils – these are pure and the highest quality
- Absolute oils – these have more of the whole plant in them
- Industrial grade oils – these are the lowest quality

Industrial grade oils have usually been hastily distilled at high temperatures. They have often also been chemically altered with synthetic solvents to generate a greater yield and, therefore, more profit. These solvents can burn the skin and make using the oils unsafe. As the chemical compounds of their constituents are rendered useless during the processing, they are mainly used by the perfume industry, rather than for healing.

Unfortunately, the market is unregulated, and industrial grade essential oils are widely available at low cost. So before purchasing oils, do your homework: phone the company you are buying from and ask if their products are therapeutic grade. You get what you pay for—the higher the cost, the better the quality. The oil should smell fresh, as though you have the plant with you.

Variables accounting for the difference in price include:
- Availability of the plant
- Cultivation methods

- Harvesting processes
- Yield
- Technique used for extracting the oil

There is a lot of misinformation about essential oils to be found on the internet, spread through ignorance and hearsay, including the belief that essential oils are toxic to animals, especially cats. It is true that cats do not have the necessary enzymes to break down essential oils, which is why care needs to be taken when working with cats. Toxicity occurs through inappropriate administration and accidental ingestion.

The Effects of Essential Oils

A plant may contain between 400 and 500 different constituents, depending on factors like weather, type of soil, and level of stress the plant is exposed to. The essential oils that are extracted from them may then contain as many as 100 different chemical components, so it's not surprising that they can have a strong effect on a person or an animal.

Their chemistry is complex, but generally includes alcohols, esters, ketones, cineole, and valarienc acid. Each essential oil contains a different mix of constituents and trace elements and has a different effect, depending on which component is predominant. For example, some oils are relaxing and soothing, while some relieve pain. Others, such as lemon and lavender, are "adaptogenic," meaning they adapt to whatever role your body needs them to fulfill.

Although the mechanism by which these essential oils act on us is not very well understood, what is clear is that they affect our mind, body, and emotions in specific ways.

So How Do They Work?

When an essential oil is inhaled through the nose, it binds to the mucous membranes of the nose, moves from the nasal passages via the bloodstream into the lungs, heart, and liver, then gets sent via the bloodstream to wherever it is needed.

Animals select essential oils in different ways:

- Inhalation – smelling
- Ingestion – licking
- Sublingual – prefer licking with the underside of the tongue
- Topical – application to the skin

The practitioner offers the extracts, and the selection thereof is done by the animal, as they intuitively determine what their bodies need and require. Each essential oil contains an individual combination of active ingredients, which the animal intuitively recognizes and chooses to self-medicate, irrespective of whether it's an emotional issue or physical condition. When physically ill or under stress the chemical receptors in the brain are altered, so the animal will gravitate toward more bitter compounds and medicinal extracts to what it usually feeds on.

As essential oils release volatile oil molecules, these active ingredients interact with the body's chemistry. Inhaling an oil allows it to be absorbed at a much faster rate than if it is ingested, where it first needs to travel to the stomach to be broken down and absorbed into the bloodstream.

Sometimes the oil is mixed in a carrier oil or gel and applied topically to areas of the body, such as when there is inflammation—all the time guided by the animal, of course. When essential oils are used topically, they are absorbed through the skin and can treat underlying muscles not just the skin.

The exact properties of essential oils, how they work, and how they interact with cells in the body is the subject of ongoing research and could be an entire book. What we do know is essential oils affect communication among the cells of the body, as well as hormones in the bloodstream and even DNA, which means they can be very potent medication.

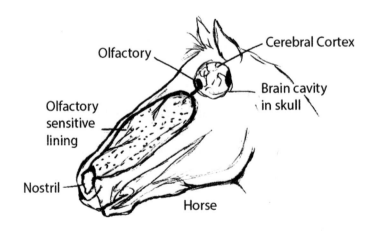

Figure 49: Olfactory Sensitive Lining (Horse)

The part of the anatomy that processes smell is called an olfactory sensitive lining in a horse and a nasal epithelium in a dog. Both can be found on the upper jaw all along the nose, and in Figure 49, you can see just how large they are.

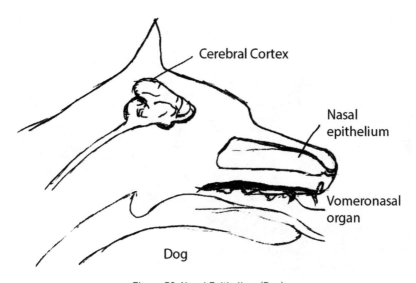

Figure 50: Nasal Epithelium (Dog)

Horses have millions of nerve cells in the olfactory receptors and when they sniff, they intensify the currents of air in the nasal passages. The odor molecules then contact the receptor cells and analyze the smell. Like humans, horses alternate the task of breathing between their two nostrils, and they often have a more dominant side, which they sometimes prefer using when offered essential oils.

Horses also have another olfactory system under the floor of their nasal cavity called the Jacobson's organ. When they lift their upper lip and show their gums, they expose all the olfactory receptors to the scent they are detecting, just like King is doing in Figure 51 on the following page. This is called the Flehman response.

The level of information horses receive about the world around them is phenomenal. They can identify possible threats using scent alone. For example, even a domesticated horse will smell a snake long before they see it, and a mare who has just given birth is able to identify her foal by scent and distinguish her offspring from others in the herd. If you were to remove a horse's olfactory lining and open it up, it would spread over the entire body of the horse. A human olfactory lining is the size of two A2 pieces of paper. As humans, we fail miserably in the olfactory department, probably because we don't rely on it for our survival as much as an animal does.

Figure 51: Flehman Response

As humans with limited olfactory abilities, it's difficult for us to understand just how well animals can smell complex chemical messages in the air, and how much their world revolves around this. This also means that essential oils have an even more powerful effect on them than they do on humans.

Aromatherapy vs Zoopharmacognosy

Aromatherapy is different from zoopharmacognosy: aromatherapy is intended exclusively for humans, while zoopharmacognosy is exclusively for animals.

The two are used and applied in distinct ways. For example, you should never consider giving your animal a massage with oils. Not only would you make their coat dirty, but you would be forcing a remedy on them, possibly causing great distress, rather than giving them the opportunity to walk away.

Self-Selection

Before animals were domesticated, they roamed free and kept themselves healthy by grazing on a large variety of different plants. They instinctively sought out the plants they needed to maintain their health or to correct it in times of illness. In fact, the basis of our herbal knowledge for humans has been acquired by watching animals seek out certain plants, according to their needs at the time.

Zoopharmacognosy gives domesticated or captive animals the opportunity to self-medicate by offering them a variety of plant extracts. These extracts contain constituents that are the same as, or similar to, those that would have been found in an animal's natural environment but which they now might not have access to. The practice allows an animal to self-select medicinal plants, thereby managing its own health. Once an animal has selected its remedy, it will then guide the session by inhaling it, taking it orally, or rubbing its body against it, depending on the remedy.

I always include self-selection in my sessions, as I truly believe in it. Watching the animal's response and behavior changes during and after a session has been incredibly rewarding.

South Africa tends to have a volatile currency, so some of the remedies I need in my kit have become astronomically expensive over the years. Because of my interest in gardening and herbs, the obvious way around this was to get creative; that is, start growing herbs and making my own infusions. Over the years, I have managed to source a variety of plants that I use on a regular basis, in the process learning more about them.

Animals sometimes show me what they need, even before it is offered to them, and because of my knowledge of plants and supplements, I can now often identify what they are talking about, even though they don't know (or even use) the word for it.

My understanding of the medicinal uses of local plants has soared in the past few years as whenever they show me a plant I don't yet know, I search for it and then try to work out why it was selected.

Although animals obviously don't know the constituents or active ingredients of the plants, or what those do, they instinctively know it will work for them. When there is an imbalance in the body, chemical changes take place in the brain, and they naturally gravitate toward more bitter plants. For example, horses sometimes eat the bark of the white willow tree. This contains a constituent called salicin which is an anti-inflammatory (and in fact, the main ingredient of aspirin).

Humans experience this, too. For example, when you start to feel ill, you don't always want to eat the same foods you normally do. In the same way, animals begin to look for and graze on plants they know will help them feel better. Interestingly, this knowledge is passed down through the mother or the herd.

As an owner, you may notice your animal wants to eat a certain plant that is not normally part of their diet. Unless you already know it is safe, before you let them eat it, first look up the plant, and research the medicinal properties to try and understand why your animal is showing an interest in it. This can tell you a lot about how your animal is feeling and what it needs.

My Kit Being Investigated

CASE STUDY: Tolero – A Dietary Supplement Request

I was working with a horse called Tolero and he asked me to mention to his owner that he loves to forage on a certain type of plant found in the surrounding Tokai forest. Apparently they hadn't visited this spot for quite some time, and he was keen to go back. From his description, the plant looked like a fungus or mushroom of some kind. Although I had heard of elephants eating reishi mushrooms in the Knysna forest, I had no idea that horses would self-select such a plant.

So it was with some trepidation that I conveyed the message to his owner, Karena, and to my astonishment she knew exactly what he was referring to. It was a mushroom that grows in the Tokai forest on the borders of his paddock. I was doing the reading going into mid-summer, and due to the unusually dry winter of 2015 (the Western Cape has its rainfall season in winter), the mushrooms had not been as prolific as in previous years so he had missed his annual graze.

Karena promised Tolero that as soon as the first rains fell to mark the start of winter, she would take him to forage on his much loved (and healthy) mushrooms. Luckily for me, she had already identified the fungus and was able to share the names: Stereum hirsutum and Lactarius deliciosus.

Lactarius Deliciosus

The common name for this is orange/saffron milk cap or red pine mushroom. It is common in pine plantations, of which South Africa has quite a few, and is found under the trees, covered in pine needles. The mushrooms usually appear from April to September and are edible and very tasty. The mushroom has antioxidant and antimicrobial properties.

Figure 52: Lactarius Deliciosus   Figure 53: Stereum Hirsutum

Other species of animals such as elephants, have been found to also eat medicinal mushrooms. In stool samples taken from the elephants in Knysna, South Africa, Gareth Patterson documents elephants eating a tree fungus known as Ganoderma applantum. This variety of mushroom contains antiviral, antibacterial and anti-parasitic properties. Primates have also been recorded to eat the delicacy.

Stereum Hirsutum

The common name for this mushroom is hairy crustcap or hairy curtain crust, and it is widely found across Southern Africa, usually on oak and eucalyptus tree stumps. Due to its tough consistency it's inedible for humans, but horses have much bigger teeth and can bite into and eat them. This fungus has antioxidant properties.

Toxicity

Occasionally animals eat things when you would think they should know better. There can be a variety of reasons for this. For example, dogs have been known to eat anti-freeze because the chemicals confuse their senses and/or they don't recognize the scent. Horses can overdose on ragwort, and wild animals may eat things they normally wouldn't if there is a lack of grazing and they are extremely hungry. In cases like this in nature, an animal would usually be able to self-medicate by eating clay from the soil, which counteracts toxins.

Why Horses Forage for Mushrooms

Mushrooms have a network of roots called the mycelium, which allows them to share nutrients and to fight bacteria and disease. For centuries, horses all over the world have been seen to eat this powerful part of the mushroom, if they are given the opportunity to graze under the right conditions. Recently, mushrooms have been used to treat horses for many different ailments, as well as to keep them generally healthy. Each type has specific properties. For example, the reishi mushroom has adaptogenic benefits that can help horses process their stress better.

In general, mushrooms contain huge quantities of antioxidants, vitamins, and enzymes. They also have their own immune system and naturally produce antibiotics, which can prevent illness. After this session I went on a mushroom foraging workshop to learn about them as much as I could. What I learned is that to identify mushrooms is not as easy as it looks and that you can easily make a mistake, so it is well worth carrying a pocket guide and looking up the mushroom before you pick it. The ones you can eat, especially the pine rings, are delicious and I can certainly understand now why horses would choose to eat them.

NOTE: Please be very careful with mushrooms and should your animal show an interest in any, be sure to research them before you let them eat any. Some mushrooms are incredibly poisonous and a small piece can be fatal. Should you wish to know more, an excellent book to read on this subject is *Wild Health* by Cindy Engel.

Healing with Essential Oils

Essential oils seem to be able to find keyholes in the consciousness of an animal, unlock the chakra needing healing, and go in and assist that healing on a much deeper level than usually experienced.

NOTE: Illustrations in the following case studies reflect the "final" destination of the oil in the body, after inhalation.

CASE STUDY: Hero – Sadness

We were working with Hero, a gelding who had experienced a lot of sadness due to moving yards throughout his life and in the process losing many close friendships he had made. Although the sadness didn't show up directly in his heart chakra, he stored it just next to it. When he inhaled the rose and neroli oils, he also moved into them and wanted them rubbed onto his chest, which I did. This released all the pent-up feelings, and the healing continued for some time, during which he inhaled, then moved away to process, before coming back to continue inhaling, several times over.

As you can see in Figure 54, the sadness first appeared as a purple haze. After he had inhaled the oil for several minutes, the color gradually changed to a nice pink, which was flowing outwards, much like in Figure 56.

Figure 54: Hero's Sadness

CASE STUDY: Princess – Inflammation

Sometimes I will see a horse after a visit from the physiotherapist, or before it. In the case of Princess, when I did an auric body scan I found that she had two tight balls or knots imbedded in her upper thigh on each leg. In this session, I had come in after the physio-therapist and had not been told he had been or what he had picked up. He had apparently worked on the area, so she was still a little sore. In our session, Princess was able to guide and determine with self-selection what she needed to help those knots in her thigh disappear completely. Her nerve endings in that area also looked dead, and she chose a remedy to correct that. She selected a mix of valerian, arnica, German chamomile, and melissa to go into a gel mix, which was then applied to the area where the red balls were found. (I now carry chalk in my kit and mark the affected area on the body so that the owners can apply the gel, as sometimes they are unsure or have forgotten the exact area they need to apply it to.) Princess also asked the stable manager to please massage her in the specified area to stimulate and rejuvenate those nerve endings.

In addition, Princess selected all of my licorice root and dried chamomile flowers, 250ml of comfrey, and 200ml of St John's wort macerated oil, confirming for me that the area was still tender and sore. This is what could be seen in her field:

Figure 55: Area of Inflammation and Release

CASE STUDY: Sadness and Loss

This was another horse that was struggling with feelings of sadness and loss as a result of losing past owners and friends. The oil he chose to help him with this process was angelica root, also known as the Oil of Angels. He absolutely loved it and simply stood quietly with his eyes closed, inhaling the fragrance. As you can see in Figure 56, the oil activated the heart chakra and he was able to let go of the sadness that had been manifesting in his heart area.

Figure 56: Activated Heart Chakra

CASE STUDY: Ally – Anxiety

Ally was a beautiful mare who had trouble settling. Although she wasn't necessarily nervous, she was always overly aware of everything going on around her and experienced a prevailing sense of anxiety.

I offered her angelica root to help instill a sense of calm. Upon inhalation, it tickled her nose on both sides of the sinuses, extending up to beneath her eyes. I picked this up as a tingling sensation in my left arm. She released the sensation by rubbing her face on anything she could find, including the door frame, the raised cement feeding trough, and me.

Sometimes when working with the oils, I feel either emotionally or physically when a major shift has happened in the animal. This helps to guide me on the type of session needed and what oils to use. For Ally, this was an emotional release, which really opened her up to healing. She was able to settle down, and we could continue with the session after that.

This raised a question: surely all emotions are stored in the heart area? Apparently not. Dr. Mona Lisa Schulz is a neuropsychiatrist and medical intuitive who wrote the book *Awakening Intuition* (Harmony, 1999). In the book, Schulz discusses how psychological issues affect the seven chakras. "From an emotional point of view, sinusitis, bronchitis, and asthma are fourth chakra or heart issues, and have to do with unexpressed or unresolved emotions."

So by rubbing her face, Ally was releasing the unexpressed emotions that she could not deal with in her heart.

Figure 57: Ally's Unexpressed Emotions

CASE STUDY: Ally – Linden Blossom for Trauma

Animals aren't the only ones affected by essential oils; humans are, too. We have used essential oils for centuries for a variety of conditions, with some remedies being discovered entirely by accident. My own theory is that if you need a certain oil to assist with healing, you will find a way to get it into your body, whether you do this consciously or not.

Ally, the mare I mentioned previously, does not like men in general, from grooms to trainers and owners. She regularly tries to kick male grooms, so they are all wary when working around her. In the reading session we did after working with the oils, she revealed that she had endured trauma to the right side of her body. She associated this with a male, who was at the time trying to "sort her out." This was great validation for us, as Melana had seen this, and I had felt it.

Linden blossom is generally offered to animals who are wary of men, as well as those who have experienced physical trauma or some form of abuse.

I obviously needed to open the bottle for Ally to sniff and therefore automatically inhaled the oil myself. The oil traveled straight to my heart area and worked its magic, activating my heart chakra. It also connected me to Ally, without me having to actively focus on this. As I mentioned earlier, I usually only consciously connect after I have worked with the oils. At the time, I was going through a traumatic and painful divorce, so in retrospect, I needed this healing as much as Ally did.

Figure 58: Linden Blossom Magic

When Ally inhaled the linden blossom, it entered her system as green (healing energy), moving through her nose and along the upper midsection of her body, finally settling on the righthand-side rump. You would think that because she had suffered abuse she would have stored that abuse or hurt in her heart, and maybe she did. But in the session, she chose to direct the healing to the physical part of her that had been hurt as a result of a man. The right side is associated with male energy, and the traumatized area immediately accepted this healing.

It's amazing how these oils work!

CASE STUDY: Emotional Release: Rose and Frankincense Oils

This horse had been separated from someone he once loved very much, as have 90 percent of all animals. Whenever a bond is severed between mother and child, or a much-loved childhood friend, this is traumatic and stays in an animal's mind forever.

In this case, there were two stages of healing and two different oils were selected.

As soon as I opened the rose oil, he moved closer to get more of the aroma. When I held out the bottle, he pressed his nose into it, and simply stood still with his eyes closed. When it entered the heart area, it immediately activated his heart chakra to begin the healing process. In this instance, all his emotion was stored in his heart, not next to it as with some of the other animals I have worked with. We are all different in the way we process our emotions, and animals are, too. When emotions are released from the physical body, they move back to wherever they came from. So essentially, in all healing, what has stepped down through the different auric layers to the physical must go back out in the same way.

As the horse's chakra was activated, it started to swirl, then all that stored emotion traveled out of the heart, through the head, and back into the aura.

He then selected frankincense essential oil, which is an unusual combination with rose, especially at the beginning of a session. Frankincense is considered a spiritual oil, which is why it is used in religious ceremonies around the world. It is usually offered to animals who are highly strung or who seem fearful, as it has a way of calming the mind. The combination of rose and frankincense assists animals in passing from the physical into the spiritual plane.

In this instance, the emotion not only moved out of his body in its entirety but in fact moved to a different level of consciousness, a higher emotional level.

Horses give off a clear frequency that is different from that of cats and dogs. I know that some people will disagree with this statement, but in my experience, horses do not have that much emotional desire to please humans, as they simply don't have to. Domesticated dogs and cats are more emotionally driven, as they live with us and share our lives far more than horses can do. Because of this, horses have evolved in ways that dogs and cats have not, and I would definitely put them on a higher level of consciousness. This does not mean that they are higher in status; it simply means that they are different. They have access to a higher emotional level, and their spirit/soul consciousness manifests more clearly.

Figure 59: Emotional Release

CASE STUDY: Hero – Self-Acceptance

When this oil was selected, it activated Hero's crown chakra. In Figure 60, you can see a flow of energy starting from the center of the body, moving up through the different levels of the aura and into the cosmos. The words "I am what I am, and that is okay" came through telepathically. Hero is very aptly named. He is one of the most lovable horses around, a true example of total self-acceptance, which is something many of us humans can only dream of.

Once or twice a year, I see this total acceptance of self in older horses, even without the frankincense oil. When I experience it, my heart chakra is overwhelmed, and I need to step away for a few minutes to process the intensity of my emotions.

Figure 60: Self-Acceptance

CASE STUDY: A Bad Castration

When I did an auric body scan on this horse, I immediately picked up that whoever had done his castration had done a terrible job, which affected him emotionally and physically. There was a dark cloud of blocked energy in the area just above his penis.

When I offered the buchu essential oil (which is not a very common selection), he displayed the flehman curl when inhaling and exposed the nerve endings on his upper lip to the oil molecules in the essential oil.

I originally offered him this oil as now and then, he tended to buck in an uncharacteristic way while being ridden. A saddle and rider would put pressure on the kidneys, and buchu is known to help the kidneys. Instead, the oil helped heal the trauma that had been created around his penis.

Figure 61: Healing Trauma to the Genital Area

CASE STUDY: Anger

When I got to the stables, I found that this was a horse who was incredibly cross with his owner for several reasons. He had heard that I was coming (gossip travels very fast in most paddocks) and had worked himself into a state to reflect his anger. He was kicking the wall, very restless turning in circles all the time, and snorting. The owner has two horses, and he felt that she was devoting more of her time to another younger horse instead of to him, so he was experiencing a big bout of jealousy. He also did not like his stable, as it was on a corner; he wanted to return to his old stable!

Figure 62: Anger

My first goal in this session was to let him voice why he was so unhappy and be supportive of what he said. Secondly, he needed to calm down physically before he hurt himself or anyone else. The red energy that you see coming of his chest in Figure 62 is the anger he was feeling. I started off with a range of emotionally supportive oils and calming oils.

Over a period of two hours, he finally calmed and settled down. The kicking and snorting stopped, and his energy shifted and was calmer. I would have to say that in this case it was a combination of the oils and getting his emotional anger off his chest and voicing it to his owner. His main selection for this session was vetiver, valerian, hops, angelica root, rose, and jasmine.

By the end of the session, the red rays had faded and his heart chakra had been restored to a nice pink color.

CASE STUDY: Storm – Sexual Abuse and Violet Leaf

There are times when I really don't enjoy my job, simply because I see the damage and maliciousness of human behavior and the harm it brings to animals. Unfortunately, drugs are a very real problem and a threat to humans as much as they are to animals. The drug tik (the South African street name for methamaphine) is more potent and damaging to the mind than any other drug. It is cheap and easy to come by and, therefore, twice as dangerous. It destroys brain cells, and when taken, it seems to induce irrational thinking and bizarre behavior in some people. Every now and then, I get to work with an animal that has suffered a great deal at the hands of humans taking tik, and what they do to animals while on tik is devastating.

One such case was a beautiful gelding called Storm. He had been bought from the SPCA nine months ago. One morning, the staff at the SPCA had arrived to find two horses waiting for them patiently outside. That type of behavior spoke volumes, so they let them in, and in the months that followed tried to find homes for them. Sometimes, lost animals will find and seek out a human that they know will help them and know what to do to help. The first time I was called to see him was by a rider who was helping to exercise him. Certain behavioral issues warranted a session—he never stood still when mounted, was extremely sensitive on his rear hind legs, and refused to leave the yard although he had been there nine months. When led down the driveway, he started breathing deeply, sweating profusely, rearing, and trying to turn back.

In session, Storm explained some of the scarring I could clearly see and pick up on his back hind quarters, some inflammation in his shoulder, and then we worked with the heart issues of which he had plenty. Some of the oils he selected were rose, neroli, linden blossom, sandalwood, and about half a bottle of violet leaf, which he had orally and wanted topically put onto his heart chakra. He explained that he did not want to leave the yard and was extremely fearful that he would be made to go back to the SPCA and his old owners (who had pitched up at the SPCA two weeks after they had left him there, trying to claim him back). I reassured him and explained that the road led to a vineyard close by where he could canter and explore to his heart's content, and that never again would he go back to his old owners. He was safe and well protected now.

In this session, he didn't go into too much detail about his past; he just selected plenty of emotional oils and anti-inflammatories to help his shoulder. I didn't push him for any more information, but I knew by the time I left that he had been sexually abused and violated through his sheath and anally by humans high on tik. I gained this knowledge psychically and using high-sense perception. I did not talk to him or ask him about it; when he was ready, he would tell me. Right now, just selecting the oils and speaking to someone who could hear him and understood was enough; I did not want to rush the progress we had made by trying for release in the session. It was the main reason he had left where he was and sought out humans who could help him.

There was a great shift in Storm after our first session, and he had an incredible turnaround. Two days after his session, he had walked down the drive and left the property, walking around the block with a little nervousness but nothing like he had displayed before. He started interacting more with his riders. He listened and continued to allow the gel mix to be applied to his cheek and the other one to his shoulder. There was a confidence about him now that had not been there before.

I was called back for a follow-up session by his new owner, who wanted to know what had happened to her horse. She had formed a close emotional bond with him and had a suspicion as to what had happened but wanted it confirmed. Again, he selected large amounts of emotional and behavioral oils (such as sandalwood to assist with fear and anxiety). I scanned the area around his sheath, and it felt dead with stagnant energy. I then attentively began sharing with his owner all that I had picked up from the first session and this session. Unfortunately, it confirmed her suspicions, and she told me that right after he had arrived from the SPCA they had discovered an infection in his sheath that required treatment. She had also noticed that he never let his penis hang when urinating, and he never urinated in front of her, except for one day, when she saw it briefly. He had growths all over his penis. She immediately called the vet, who had to examine him under sedation. He was immediately booked in for an operation where 75 percent of the penis had to be removed due to cancerous growths. The vet had also found a huge amount of scarring on the inside of the sheath, which he could not explain.

Because I am human and some other human had inflicted this terrible harm, I felt I needed to apologize to Storm for their actions. I took some time in explaining in my own way why I was deeply sorry that this had happened to him, that not all humans are the same, and so on. He listened and then just walked over and hung his head on my neck, consoling me, when I was trying to console him. Not once did he say a thing; his actions spoke louder than words.

When I asked Storm how he felt now, he gave this huge sigh of relief and simply stated that the part of him that had suffered the most had now been removed so he had been able to make a new beginning. A traumatic event stays with an animal or human for the rest of their lives, and although he will never forget what happened, he has been able to put it behind him and embrace a new life. This reading will stay with me for the rest of my life. The wisdom and forgiveness Storm has shown to the human race is something we can all learn from.

CASE STUDY: Pony – Past Abuse

Pony has past abuse issues from his earlier years as a cart horse, and although he has made a full recovery over several years, there are areas in his body where he is very sensitive. If you do an auric body scan you can pick it up, specifically in his head area and on one or two of his lower legs. In previous sessions, he has never really wanted to reveal too much about his past abuse, preferring to share more about life in the present. However, in this session, I once again scanned the same area and decided to offer him some cornflower water, which he inhaled and choose to lick several times.

Cornflower water opens an animal up to healing and is usually offered at the start of the session. I felt he wanted more than just inhaling the water, so I moved to his legs, specifically those where he had experienced the abuse, and gently sprinkled cornflower water on them. There was a subtle shift in his energy, so to help move it to the next level, I offered him some violet leaf essential oil. Violet leaf is offered to animals with unpleasant experiences as it comforts the heart.

Figure 63: Healing Past Abuse Issues

As soon as he started inhaling the violet leaf, his energy shifted dramatically. At one point, I tried to move away to let him process things on his own, but he moved with me. I realized that I was supporting his healing, so I let it continue. At first his auric field was a little dull, as is typical of a horse who has suffered past abuse. As the minutes ticked by, his field became filled with slivers of silver and his aura gradually became brighter. I became emotional in a relieved, happy way as his energy changed. We stood transfixed for a while and then, with a deep sigh, he moved away from me and the oil. The cornflower water and violet leaf had done their job. It was the first time I had experienced and seen such a tangible shift on an emotional level, a privilege I was fortunate to be included in.

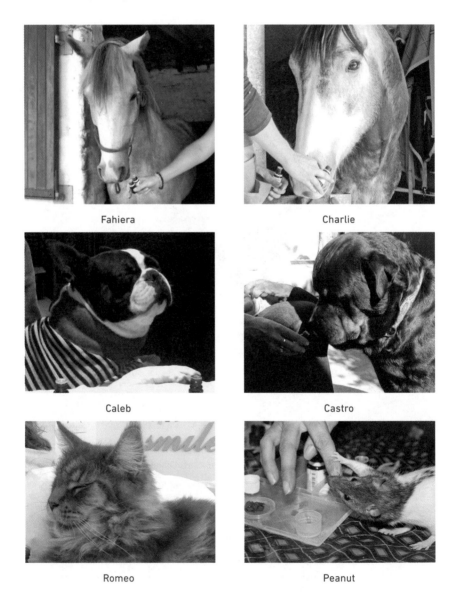

Fahiera

Charlie

Caleb

Castro

Romeo

Peanut

6

High-Sense Perception

High-sense perception (HSP) is a term not many people understand, so I have included this chapter to give you an idea of what a psychic or intuitive might see when using HSP to work with an animal.

When I'm working with an animal, either in a reading or healing session, it really helps to be able to see what's happening energetically in the body without having to resort to surgery. It's also useful to get a heads-up on something; for example, when a mare comes into season, her womb changes.

I am not a vet, so all I can do is explain my perception of what I am seeing. This has been a personal learning curve for me, as I have often not understood. Sometimes I can work it out by explaining it in detail to the owner, so that they can confirm what the animal has struggled with in the past (or present). Other times, I've needed to hit the books after a session, or use Google, to try to understand what I've been shown. Luckily, I enjoy investigating and solving problems, so if I am being shown something, then I want to understand why and what it means. My job and my clients are constantly changing, and I learn something new every day. And the more I learn and explore the physical body, both inside and out, the more my knowledge expands and the better reader and interpreter I can be.

Something to remember, though, is that if an animal does not want you to know what's going on, they will not show it to you, and that is their right. Sometimes if they have experienced a deep trauma or injury, you first need to gain their trust before they will reveal that to you for healing, and that doesn't always happen in the first session. Other times, there are so many things going on, it's simply a case of prioritizing what healing is needed most urgently, whether emotional, physical, or mental.

Ligaments

CASE STUDY: Tinkerbell

Tinkerbell is a seven-year-old mix of Ragdoll and Abyssinian feline bloodlines. She had recently fallen and hurt herself, and due to this she was limping. Her owners, Anneliza and Vernon, wanted to offer her a self-selection session to support her naturally, then an animal communication session to find out what else they could do to help.

When I connected with her, she showed me how she had hurt her foot. It had been raining all week, and she wanted to jump onto the patio wall, which gave her a better vantage point over the garden. The top of the wall was so wet from the rain, though, she had not been able to grip as she would normally do. She landed back on her feet on the ground, which was also wet, and her right foot slipped out and twisted.

I first offered her a variety of oils and macerates to help her settle and reduce any pain. She finally settled down on top of the bed, so I sat next to her and held my hand close to, but not touching, the area that was sore. She first showed me where on her foot she had hurt herself, then she went a little deeper and showed me exactly what needed to be done.

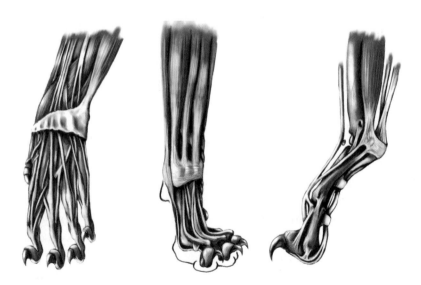

Figure 64: Internal View of a Cat's Claw

If you look at the middle picture in Figure 64 on the previous page, the ligaments traveling from the toes upward (the dorsal elastic ligaments) were torn. Her ligaments looked like the image in Figure 65 below. It wasn't a severe tear; just a few fraying strands.

Figure 65: Analogy for the Torn Ligament

To assist the healing, Tinkerbell specifically requested a coil wrapped around each tendon, as per the image in Figure 66 below.

Figure 66: Healing Coil

During the healing session, I saw each ligament individually, and as the healing progressed, the coil gradually tightened up to support the ligament better, becoming thicker and merging to become like a solid rope again. The entire process of surrounding each ligament with light and then "coiling" it took about 15 minutes. She didn't move once during this time. By the time the healing was finished, she was in a deeply relaxed state and didn't even move when we got off the bed and left the room.

That evening she chose St John's wort macerated oil and had a little arnica oil, too. The next day, she was much better and bearing weight on the foot again. After that, she didn't choose any further remedies as she clearly didn't need them.

Tinkerbell

PMS

CASE STUDY: Penny Whistle

Most women have heard of or experienced some form of premenstrual syndrome (PMS). For humans, this can show up in a wide variety of symptoms, such as mood swings, tender breasts, food cravings, fatigue, irritability, and depression. The physical and emotional changes different women experience can vary from just noticeable all the way up to intense.

I had never really given much thought to the possibility that animals might experience PMS too until I started coming into contact with mares who suffer from it.

Mares can become very temperamental and moody one to two weeks before their season begins. Through the use of high-sense perception, this can be seen clearly in their cervix and vagina. The womb wall becomes whitish/pinkish, and it seems to swell a little in preparation for this phase of fertility. The mares are usually very aware of it and don't mind showing it to you.

My first experience of this was when I was working at a livery stable. I was waiting for an owner and horse to finish up with the vet, who had dropped by unexpectedly, so I had time on my hands. I decided to check up on another client's mare, who I had worked with before. We exchanged pleasantries and, boy, she wasn't in a good mood at all.

First, she was irritated with the geldings in the paddock next door, who were behaving like most young geldings. They had been running around chasing each other all day and showing off, which they were still doing at the time of the conversation. I laughed at this and asked her if perhaps she didn't want to run around with them. "No way!" was the immediate response. She was clearly highly irritated that I could even ask that question!

Next on her list of grievances was the fact that her food had been changed and she wasn't happy about that. And the list went on. Just as I was about to move off to begin the session I was there for, as the vet had now finished, she showed me her cervix. It was a pinkish color and looked puffy and swollen, and she told me she would come into season within a week or two. Then the penny dropped! She was premenstrual, with all the classic irritability symptoms felt by humans. She taught me a valuable lesson as she did in fact come into season the following week, and her mood improved dramatically after that.

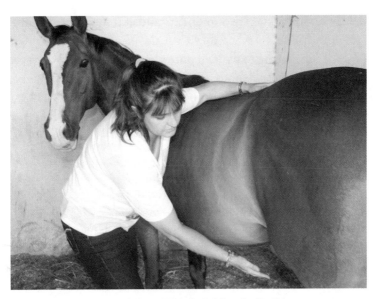

Figure 67: Penny Whistle Guiding the Healing

I have worked with other mares since then, and some of them experience intense PMS. They tell me that they really suffer and their lower stomach aches, just like a human woman's does. They may moan with pain and discomfort, and some of them even lie down to try and ease it.

If you suspect this may be happening with your mare, be aware that her lower stomach is probably sore. Avoid touching that area or you might be kicked. And if she is a bit moody, especially when you tighten the girth, she has good reason to be, so take it easy or give her the day off.

A last note on mares: Some owners of mares are unsure whether or not their mares have carried a foal. When meeting a mare, do a scan using high-sense perception and "see into" the cervix, noting whether it is stretched and the muscles have a loose, white, elongated look to them, as this can tell you whether she was pregnant at some stage. The mare can also tell you whether she has been pregnant before if you do a connection before the scan.

Mothers Milk

I will never forget one of the mares I did a session with. I was standing next to the mare while doing the reading, and the owner was standing in front, holding her daughter, who must have been about four or five months old at the time. I had the sudden craving for milk (and I don't drink milk), so I knew this was not me but the mare and involved an issue around milk. I voiced the thought and tried to understand and interpret the meaning, as horses only drink milk when they are foals. We stood there for a full two minutes, with me trying to figure it out, when I saw the baby lowering her head in an attempt to latch onto her mother, as a breastfed baby sometimes does. A flood of intense emotions hit me from the mare as she watched. The scene and the smell of milk had reminded her of her own foal, whom she loved very much (as all moms do).

Unhappy Tummy

CASE STUDY: Ice

Ice is a beautiful white pony who is 18–20 years old and the favorite at a local riding school. She has an easy-going temperament and loves the attention she gets from all the children.

When I started working with her, I had to start the reading the moment I entered the stall as she literally took "the reins." She was so happy that someone could finally hear her that she just dived in. She came across as cheeky, with a good sense of humor, and she knew exactly who she was, how far she had come in life, and the work she had done to get there.

After a while she slowed down and became more settled. So before offering her any plant extracts, I let her "catch her breath" and quickly did a scan of her energy field. A few past injuries came up, but as I moved my hands under her belly, I became aware of discomfort in her stomach and saw what looked like empty straws or worms. I suddenly got very nauseous and needed to move away to try and settle the feeling.

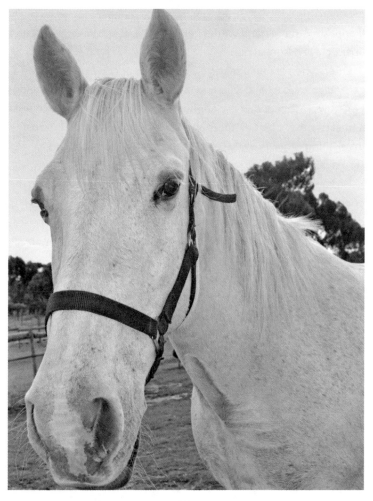

Ice

Wanting to double-check that it was her giving me the nausea and not my own body, I went back and held my hand over that area again. The nausea returned but not as bad, so I knew it was her not me. As I've mentioned, animals can sometimes pass an emotion or physical symptom on to us when we do a body scan. I allow this to happen as it helps me to better understand what's happening and to pass the information on to the owner. Sometimes they then need to call in the vet, farrier, or dentist to take a deeper look at what's going on.

Now that I had a sense of how Ice was feeling, I could move on to plant extracts that might help her. She chose dried wormwood (Wilde Als), which is a common selection for worms, and finished my entire tub of about 300g. She then took ginger essential oil orally (I applied it to my hand with a neutral oil, and she licked it off) and finally clove essential oil.

Often when animals select clove, ginger, or garlic essential oil, it can indicate a bacterial infection in the stomach. Added to the selection of wormwood, it was clear her tummy was not happy. I offered a host of other plant extracts after this, but she was not interested in anything other than the extracts she had already chosen for her stomach.

Half an hour later, I went back to the area of the colon to see if the energy had shifted after the extracts she had selected. I was looking down at the floor, focusing my eyes on nothing in particular and just paying attention to her stomach, when the area around my shoes glowed green, beaming down from her stomach. Green energy indicates healing and was a lovely confirmation of what had happened.

Another bucket of water (next to her normal drinking bucket) was put in her paddock and a few drops of clove and ginger essential oil added to it, so she could carry on selecting for the next few hours if she needed it. The following morning there was a marked difference in the water level of the bucket, which showed the self-selection process had continued.

Implants and Surgeries

Another thing that can be picked up when doing a body scan using HSP is things in the body that have been done surgically. One such case was Taipan. When I scanned his front leg, it felt cold and looked like steel plates inside—not one but several on top of each other, like a sandwich.

Kim, his owner, explained he had had an operation for a lesion of the medial branch of suspensory ligaments, which means one line of white ligament and one line of pressed iron plates.

Other things like microchips and pins can also be picked up.

Arthritis

When scanning the body of an animal using high-sense perception, one of the easiest things to see is arthritis. If the bones are in good condition, they appear to be heavy and strong. If arthritis is present, the bones appear much lighter and tend to have many larger holes in them.

Normal Osteoporotic Bone

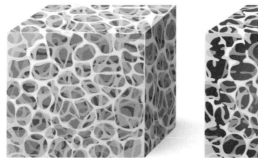

Figure 68: Arthritis

Scar Tissue

Many of us have accidents and operations, and so do our animals. When I see an area of the body that has sustained injury at some point in the animal's life, it always appears as a gray area with white surrounding tissue. If plates have been put in, I pick up silver and a foreign object. Although I never know what took place or why, I describe what I see in the body, using high-sense perception, and the owner can then confirm the accident or operation that took place.

A Note on Hooves

Horses stand for most of their lives, and their hooves and shoes are incredibly important, as they support the body. You may have had the experience yourself of wearing a new pair of shoes that pinch or are too tight; you are aware of them the entire time you are on your feet. Even if the horse is unshod, care still needs to be taken to trim the hooves correctly. The condition of their feet can have a major impact on their lives, putting them off balance or creating extreme pain, if conditions such as laminitis appear.

Even though I have no formal training as a vet or farrier, horses guide me intuitively to their feet. I then use high-sense perception and look into the foot itself. In scanning the hooves, it's also possible to pick up if something else is in the process of going wrong. For example, if the inside of the hoof walls look more hollow than normal, a little like pan pipes, and are unusually dry, the hoof then needs feeding or problems will set in.

Horses sometimes also show me what isn't working for them, or that they would like something changed in the way they are being shoed or their hooves rasped. I then pass on the message and describe what I am seeing to the owner, farrier, or groom.

There are times when a horse is extremely happy with their hooves and has nothing but praise for the farrier. Those readings are the best, as they often like to show their feet off. When I get down there, they simply laugh and tell me I will find nothing wrong in that department, then they ask if I've noticed just how lovely they are looking. Of course I agree and tell them how wonderful they look. I also make sure that I pass the message on to the owner, who hopefully tells the farrier that the message came "straight from the horse's mouth"!

CASE STUDY: Jade

I did a session on a horse called Jade and scanned her feet as usual. There was nothing wrong with the hooves or the shoes, but there was a small ball beginning to form near the point of the frog (center of the hoof) that was not supposed to be there. At that point, the mass was about the size of a 20 cent South African coin but was not causing any pain.

After I had noticed the mass, which I suspected might be an abscess, I asked the mare if she knew what it was, and she confirmed that it was the beginning of an abscess. It wasn't yet bad enough to get the farrier involved, but she asked that the owners call him out in two to three weeks.

I got a message three weeks later to let me know that the abscess had developed in the third week, and they had just had the farrier out to drain and clean it and pack it with Epsom salts. In a situation like this, it's not always fun being "right"; I would rather the horse not have the abscess and the discomfort that comes with it.

Laminitis

Laminitis is one of the most crippling diseases horses, ponies, and donkeys can suffer from. Severe and recurring cases of laminitis can reduce a horse's usefulness, or result in the horse being put to sleep to end the pain and suffering that comes with the condition.

CASE STUDY: Spirit

Spirit was a former carthorse, which in the Cape sometimes means extremely rough living conditions, uneducated owners, and trauma. However, there are also carthorse owners who love their horses and care for them to the best of their ability, and it shows. In Cape Town, the Carthorse Protection Society monitors the carthorses on the road daily and does a huge amount of work in educating and helping owners with their horses. If they do a check and find a horse being mistreated or abused, they confiscate them immediately and then often rehome them or educate the owner on how to treat the horse properly. Flint was such a rescue case, and he had severe laminitis.

Spirit

I worked with him by first offering emotional essential oils, then followed this with physical extracts. When I scanned his feet, the inflammation and pain were predominantly in the coronary band, which is located at the junction of the leg's hairline and the hoof. It provides most of the nutrition to the hoof and is the area from which the hoof grows.

I held my hand just above this band on the left side of his front hoof and ran it from left to right. The moment my hand came to the middle of the hoof, it started to ache and continued to throb until I reached the righthand side. I wasn't shown the area inside the band, as the horse simply wanted to let me know how sore it was. This was the first time I had experienced laminitis as such a physical sensation in my body, and I had to massage my hand for a few minutes afterwards to get rid of the throbbing.

He chose a variety of extracts to help with his condition. Initially, they worked, but after several weeks, his condition deteriorated and he was not improving as everyone had hoped. Sadly, the time came to call it a day, as he was in too much pain, and he was put to sleep.

Animal Healing

Animals also have their own healing abilities and often use them without us even realizing it.

CASE STUDY: Molly Helps

Molly is my basset hound. One day, I took her to the animal communication class I was teaching so that she could help with the auric perception exercise we were doing that day. One of the students was Tanya, who at the time was about six months pregnant, and she sat next to Molly to practice on her. I was watching the two of them and began to notice a lovely orange energy, which looked like an umbilical cord, extend from Molly's stomach to Tanya's pregnant belly, aiming for the left lower side of her stomach. I asked Molly what she was doing, and she showed me that the baby's foot had been causing Tanya some discomfort and Molly had just helped to ease it.

After Tanya was finished with the exercise, I asked her if she had been experiencing some discomfort in the area Molly had sent healing to. She confirmed that she had indeed been uncomfortable all day, but now that she was thinking and talking about it, the discomfort seemed to have disappeared. As a point of interest, cats can transmute negative energy more than we can, which is why you will often find a healer with a cat who sometimes enters the session to help with the healing.

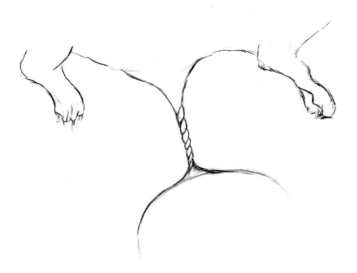

Figure 69: Molly Helps

Cancer

It is always upsetting when the Big C is mentioned, whether it be human or animal. It is almost always a foregone conclusion of the inevitable, where we have to face our own and our animal's life path. There are definitely times when chemo and other methods are an option, but at other times it is not what the animals want. In some sessions, I have smelled cancer psychically, not physically. It is a rancid damp odor and not that pleasant. I can only smell it if the animal shows or wants me to pass on the information to the owner. I have yet to detect it in humans but can certainly understand a dog's ability to sniff out cancer in urine.

7

Past Lives

Nature gives us examples of reincarnation every day. For example, the process of life and death, day and night, and the most basic of all, a plant that grows from a seed and then dies, leaving its own seeds. The wind blows, the seeds get dispersed, land on the soil, and when the time is right begin to grow, and the plant is reborn.

Reincarnation and the concept of past lives has existed for thousands of years across many cultures, from the Greeks, Asians, and Indians through to the Celtic tradition, and the concept is still prevalent today.

Whether we believe in it or not, we've all lived before, and those lives stretch beyond our ego and contribute to our development as a soul. In fact, the purpose of our soul is to learn and grow, and the cycle of evolution can be understood as a progression of consciousness through that learning and growing.

There does seem to be a general misunderstanding among people about the retrogression of past lives. It stems from understanding the way evolution works in metaphysical principles. An animal can evolve over a period of time and become a human, but a human cannot regress and go back to being an animal. The soul cannot go backwards to another level, despite the most horrendous deeds imaginable. It can, however, incarnate again (as a human) to learn the lesson it failed to learn the last time it was here.

We've chosen our current life to help us clear our karma (the result of less-than-perfect past choices), to work through certain issues, and to learn and grow further. To assist with this process, we set up soul contracts with those around us, both humans and animals. So when we say that someone comes into our life for a reason, that is very true, and it applies to animals, too.

Not every animal you have owned will have a past life connection to you. Considering how many animals those who love them will know in their lifetime, it would be presumptuous to assume such a thing. Some are special, though; perhaps because they're sometimes difficult, or they push your boundaries, or you love them so much that you cannot imagine your life without them. There might well be a past life connection with these particular animals, and even a karmic episode to be lived or life lesson that must be learned, either by us or by them.

Many people struggle to accept themselves, and it is sometimes much easier accepting love from an animal than love from another human, where fear of rejection or of being judged, or lack of self-love or self-worth get in the way. Animals teach us how to love unconditionally. They accept us for what and who we are, warts and all.

When we accept an animal in return, we open our hearts, which allows others to be invited in. This has the potential to change us and help us view things from another perspective—if we allow it. This process doesn't necessarily require a past life association; merely being associated with animals allows our consciousness to evolve and helps their evolution on a spiritual level, too.

Past Life Influences

Animals also evolve and grow through their lifetimes, and it's sometimes possible to connect into those past lives when working with them. Sometimes an animal has a physical or psychological condition that has no logical explanation if we look only at their current lives and how that animal was raised. Often, no medical or scientific reason can be found, and in cases like these, the issue may stem from a past life.

CASE STUDY: Taipan – A Grizzly Bear

Taipan is a gorgeous six-year-old gelding and a true romantic at heart. He loves everything about mares and is quite the stud around the paddock, a real Casanova. Although he is physically healthy, he tends to overexert himself, especially his hind legs, as a result of too much mounting.

Kim, his owner, confirmed that the vet had examined his hind legs on many occasions and even x-rayed the joints, but could not find anything physically wrong with them, apart from Taipan overexerting himself every now and then with the odd mare. But after hacking, he sometimes lifts his left hind leg as though it is inflamed and sore, but there is no inflammation in sight.

When I did an auric scan using high-sense perception, the joint in his back left fetlock immediately felt off. The best way I can describe it is that something felt out of place. The joint felt tight and was surrounded with a very light purple haze. This is different from how it normally looks, even if there is a physical problem, and the color purple also indicated to me that it was a spiritual or soul issue.

I placed my hands close to the area to try and get a better understanding of what was going on inside. Instead of getting an image of the joint, muscles, or ligaments, as I usually would, I felt like I had stepped into another era. These kinds of images sometimes appear in my mind's eye like a movie shown in quick flashes. I then have to piece the flashes together to try and understand what I'm seeing and then relay this to the owner.

In another lifetime, Taipan was a huge, brown grizzly bear living in North America, judging from the surrounding terrain. It was pretty cold, but the vegetation was fresh, and it looked like spring, as the ground was covered in new grass and tiny white flowers. The grizzly bear was lying injured on the edge of a forest, close to a stream, and his foot was caught in a nasty snare, which had trapped his left back ankle. After an extreme amount of pain and suffering, he passed away from his wound. He carried that injury over into his current lifetime, which also explains why the vet found nothing medically wrong with him.

I sent healing energy to the area, and while I was working on this part of his body, I offered him yarrow essential oil for the trauma experienced in his last lifetime, which had bled through to this one. When he sniffed it, his head pulled back a little, and he stared at all my bottles transfixed, before moving in for another inhalation.

Once he had had enough, I moved to the left back fetlock and applied the yarrow, as well as frankincense for spiritual issues, all around the joint. He stood quietly and raised his foot so I could have better access to the area. If at any time he had moved away or seemed uncomfortable, I would have immediately stopped. He simply sighed, though, seemingly very relaxed and enjoying the process.

When I finished, he put his foot down with all his weight on it, and the heavy energy I had originally felt around him immediately lifted.

CASE STUDY: Command and Go

Sometimes when I see past lifetimes, different time periods come up, and I'm always a little worried about whether the time period I am seeing and describing is correct. I am no history buff, so I just try to describe to the best of my ability the strange scenery, clothes, and even smells I am experiencing. I sometimes Google some of the details afterwards to better understand and confirm what I've seen. It's always so interesting to me, as I get to see what life was like in different centuries.

Command and Go is a beautiful horse who was imported all the way from Australia, and Megan is now his proud owner. He had been hacked just before I arrived for the session, and his hind legs were a little sore. He selected an array of remedies to alleviate the inflammation, including St John's wort macerated oil, arnica macerated oil and comfrey leaves.

What was so interesting here is that there was a gray mare standing next to him in his paddock. This was not actually a living, breathing horse, but one who had passed over and popped in every now and then to check up on him. They had had a very close relationship until she had passed away. When Megan asked who he missed most in the world, I got the letter S, and the moment she said Sweet Pea, he nodded in confirmation.

Command and Go also showed me a past lifetime that he and Megan had shared. It was in the late 1800s/early 1900s, when women wore long skirts to cover their ankles. I saw a scene from a typical English countryside, and Megan was a woman of high rank. She had on a long, brown, tailored skirt with short ankle boots, a stylish hat. and gloves to match. She loved her horse dearly and would ride every now and then, but was not actively involved in stabling or grooming him.

Megan's association with Command and Go in this lifetime is to learn to be more practically involved in his daily life, with his wants and needs. This was intended to encourage her to have a closer relationship with and understanding of not only her horse but any animal and human that she chooses to share her life with.

CASE STUDY: Toto – Past Trauma

Toto comes across as a very easy-going horse at first. He does everything that is expected of him, even if it is extreme and he is uncomfortable. This is not good for anyone, and especially not for a horse.

Some horses are "broken" in an extremely violent and aggressive way and/or have a really hard life. For both humans and animals, if we can't express emotions, things tend to get bottled up inside until one day they explode.

Horses show emotion in many different ways. They might be affectionate or playful or let their personality come through as we get to know them. They should also show their owners when they are unhappy or uncomfortable; for example, when a girth is too tight or they don't like their food.

When I first started actively connecting with him, Toto was stand-offish. He knew what I did and what was going on, but he wasn't really willing to open up to me. I totally understand this, and know that for some animals it can be a relief to meet someone who understands them, while others need a little time to fully open up.

I decided to start with my essential oil kit, so that I could get him to relax and get used to me physically first. After working with the oils, he was more relaxed and in a better space, and it was time to find out why he had been bottling his emotions up for most of his adult life. I knew that this was happening as it felt like my heart was about to explode. All my emotions felt trapped and could not come out. On top of this, his throat chakra was totally closed.

It turned out that there were two major reasons for this. One stemmed from an early trauma experienced as a young yearling, when he was separated from his mother for a brief period before being reunited. The second was from a past life, when he was also a horse, a very fluffy, rough type of pony, living on vast flat plains that were really cold in winter. He was part of a herd that was owned by a cruel man who kept his herd not only for transport purposes but also to eat.

If a horse gave him any hassles by not behaving as he wanted, he would threaten it with slaughter. Whether the behavior was due to lack of care or was the owner's fault was irrelevant. If it did not improve, he would beat the horse into total submission, then slaughter it in front of the herd. He then got his family to process the meat and eat it.

Centuries ago this was pretty much the norm, although the owner was usually more discreet and respectful and did the slaughtering out of sight of the other animals. In Toto's previous life, this was threatened and then carried out in front of them. Because of this, the horses dared not do anything wrong as they were all afraid they would be the next victim, then all the others would have to witness their punishment. It traumatized him to such an extent that he carried that worry through to this lifetime. As a result, he kept himself totally in check whenever he associated with humans.

I explained to Toto that times have changed and it was time to release that memory. His current owner adores him with all her heart and would never think of doing such a thing. I also explained that humans these days mainly own horses for sport, and that he could relax and enjoy himself when out riding or in the ring. It was a huge relief to him that he could now start expressing himself and stop worrying about being eaten.

This case really bought home to me the fact that as humans we can be so very cruel that an animal carries the trauma into another lifetime, and it affects them to the degree it did Toto.

8

Animals in Our Lives

This book would not be complete without some stories about animals I have communicated with. These are special and dear to me, and I hope you will enjoy reading about them as much as I enjoyed the experiences at the time.

Funnily enough, it is always the small things that come up in a reading that make it special for the owner and for me, and this is one of the reasons I love what I do.

The Role of Animals in Our Lives

To domesticate an animal means to bring them into alignment with our human desires and perspectives, which are usually very different to those of an animal. Animals in the wild live solely on instinct; without that instinct, they would be someone else's supper. Domestication also means not being completely free to roam or to even eat as they please. Pets therefore align with their humans for only one of two reasons: either by their own choice or from a place of surrender. When they do, they have a powerful impact on our lives.

Nature, including the animal world, demonstrates to the human species just what balance, alignment, and non-resistance look like. All being well, your animal has no expectations of you. Think back to when you've entered a room while your animal is relaxed and lying down. Unless you are holding food or a leash in your hand (let's get real here!), they usually stay where they are and simply watch you from the corner of their eyes, reflecting acceptance and unconditional love. These qualities of acceptance and love make us feel good as they are such powerful and high vibrations. Whenever we feel them, we come more into alignment with our higher selves, with each other, and with a higher divine source.

We actively decide to communicate with animals for a variety of reasons. It could be pure curiosity, or wanting to understand them better, or perhaps we have specific questions we want to ask, or we simply want to tell them just how much we love them—although they already know this, having always felt that love.

I have always joked that working as an animal communicator is sometimes like watching a movie. At times it feels like all I need is a box of popcorn and a slushie to complete the picture. I've often wished that other people could plug into what I am seeing, as it's sometimes frustrating that I cannot adequately describe it. Regardless, there are often tears of happiness and tears of sadness, and plenty of laughter in between from all three of us, the horse, the owner, and myself.

CASE STUDY: Brighty – Saying Goodbye

I have known Charlene for many years. Her cat Brighty had just turned 21 years old, and although 21 is a remarkable age for a cat, her health was suffering. She had always been rather thin, but now she was struggling to eat properly.

Figure 70: Brighty Leaving

She was still feisty, and her eyes showed that she was full of life, but her body just could not keep up. Charlene knew it was time to say goodbye to her beloved companion of the last 21 years, and she made the necessary arrangements to have her put down.

As I was on the road that day, I only managed to connect with Brighty an hour before the appointment with the vet. The image on the previous page, Figure 70 is what I received then, and for once I could draw what I saw. It was like she was on a stage and there was a spotlight shining down on her. The edges of the light had little specks of gold floating around and her crown chakra was activated with light streaming out. She was ready to ascend and help was at hand in the form of a loving angelic presence. I sent the image through to Charlene with a parting message from Brighty. This image really helped Charlene with the process of finally saying goodbye to her beloved cat. I hope it brings comfort to anyone who is or has been in a similar situation.

CASE STUDY: Tolero – A True Leader

One of the things I love about my job is that I never seem to stop learning about animals. Although there is sometimes a recurring theme among animals who live together, each session is totally and utterly different. Something that always stands out for me, though, is that an animal's personality and outlook on life teach everyone around them and enrich their lives, too. I will forever be grateful for the knowledge they have so readily shared with me. You cannot get that kind of wisdom and understanding from Google, that's for sure!

One such remarkable session was with Tolero, the beautiful gelding I mentioned earlier. He is stabled in Tokai Forest, Cape Town, with a herd of about 15 other horses. In fact, he was the third horse I had worked with in the herd. He is a fine fellow, with a gentle presence, and throughout the entire session he stood placidly. At times, he even nodded off, and I played with his bottom lip, teasing him to wake him up to continue our interaction. Energetically, he came across as a calm and loving horse, a dream to work with.

He is of medium build, slightly bigger than a pony, and only nine years old. Because of this and his gentle and loving nature, it came as a surprise to me when his owner mentioned that he was head of the herd. This was the first time I had ever connected with a herd leader, and I had absolutely no knowledge of how they usually behave or interact.

Apparently he is not aggressive in any way; he simply leads with a look or by using his body language, such as putting his ears back. In my humanness, I had assumed that a leader is always dominant and assertive, a typical extrovert. I had also imagined that a herd leader would have to be quite impressive in height, build, and looks—something more like a stallion. When I found out about Tolero, though, I was forced to put all my preconceived ideas aside and simply listen to him.

Tolero and Company

Because animal communication is telepathic, a reading is often a three-way conversation between me, the animal, and the owner. Tolero teased me for being surprised and scoffed at my blatant ignorance of how things in the animal kingdom were often different. I just laughed and agreed with him wholeheartedly. He led with firmness and love, and he didn't have to do or say much to let everyone around him know exactly how he felt. Frankly, it's a pity more of our human leaders are not like this horse.

Tolero mentioned that there was a particular horse in the herd he was worried about. It was a younger gray who had recently seemed to withdraw from the rest of the herd. He was keeping to himself, and this worried Tolero, as he thought he might be depressed. He mentioned that he had posted two sentries to keep an eye on him and help him through this downward turn. I was totally blown away by his concern and how he managed it.

Lastly, Tolero also felt he had to mention an incident he was not particularly happy about. He asked his owner to please *not* throw her cabbage leaves on top of the compost pile. Apparently, one of the horses in the herd had managed to get to them and chomped his way through a feast of cabbage leaves. A few hours later, his explosive farts had sent the rest of the herd gasping for fresh air and scattering to avoid standing downwind from him. Would she please be so kind as to work her cabbage leaves into the pile of compost in future, to prevent this kind of thing from happening again?

CASE STUDY: Bob – The Lover of Home-Cooked Food

Dogs love food. It's incredibly important to them, and they really love sharing this part of their lives with me. They like sharing their owner's food, and they tell me all about the food they are getting. What they like and don't like always comes up in a reading.

Bob is a lively (and spoiled!) terrier who simply adores his owner. In session, he had just one complaint about her: she didn't cook enough! He loves the smell of cooking, but instead, they often get takeout meals. After a good laugh, his owner agreed with him. She doesn't enjoy cooking, and as it's only her and her husband, they often get ready-made meals (Bob's interpretation of takeout) delivered to them. Sorry, Bob...we do understand!

CASE STUDY: Patch – The Stage Director

Not all readings are serious; some are very funny and stick in your mind for a long time. When an animal has a great sense of humor, it often comes through in a session. One such case was a horse called Patch, a beautiful white and black spotted (as per his name) 12-year-old gelding. He has a soft and loving temperament, and he particularly adores women, whether in human or horse form. For him, there is nothing in this world more beautiful than a mare whom he can lovingly gaze at; it makes his world complete.

During a session with him, I scanned his feet. Usually horses either praise their farrier or they openly dislike them. The best farriers have a loving and calm temperament. They take their time with the horse's hooves and speak gently but firmly to them while filing and shoeing is underway. If a horse has sensitive feet, though, or has perhaps had a bad experience with a farrier, there is a very good chance that they will play up when being shoed, hating the whole experience, refusing to stand still, and generally making things difficult.

Patch

Patch fell into the latter category. As soon as I reached his knee area, he told me he really did not like the way the current farrier had done his shoes. Ideally, the farrier should use a shoe that is closest to the horse's size, but often this doesn't happen. If they don't have the necessary fit with them, they tend to make do and use the next "best" fitting shoe. Patch said it felt like the farrier had tried to file his front feet to fit the shoes, not the other way around (the way he conveyed this to me had me stumbling around the paddock on tiptoes, trying to describe to the owner what he was showing me).

The farrier had cut the sides of the hoof too short, then "boxed in" the remaining hoof and filed it to fit the shoe. This was only the case with the front two hooves. It felt to me like I was walking in high heels. I had hard hiking boots on that day and haven't worn high heels in years, so my balance was totally off. I felt like a real idiot, especially with Patch laughing at my efforts. He was determined to get the message across, though, and I had to act out and describe why the shoes didn't work and how they made my feet feel. The lengths I sometimes go to, to convey a message!

At first, the owner looked at me as if I were mad, then started laughing as it finally all made sense to her, and in the end, we all had a good laugh at how ridiculous I looked. She was then able to tell me that she had suspected something was up with his shoes, and had decided two months ago not to shoe him anymore. The cheeky horse hadn't bothered to mention that the horrible shoes had already been taken off. He was too busy explaining the situation and then enjoying himself at my expense!

CASE STUDY: Hogan — I Am Not What I Appear to Be

I was doing a reading with Catherine and her dog Hogan. Hogan looks like a mix of Maltese poodle and a few other breeds. He has the typical overbite common to the Maltese breed and his bottom teeth therefore stick out. He walks with a bit of a swagger, as if to say "I am The Man," although he's a real softie, too.

His owner wanted to know if he knew what mix of breeds he was. So I asked, and his reply was "a bit of Maltese and some Labrador." Now I have worked with a lot of mixed breeds before, and since Hogan only weighs about 12kg and looks completely different to a Labrador, I questioned his answer. I told him to be serious and give me the right breeds. He still insisted that he was part-Labrador.

Our "silent" conversation continued for about five minutes, as I was sure there was no way he was a Labrador. I thought he was try-ing to make fun of me in front of his owner, which sometimes does happen, and I didn't want his sense of humor to be at my expense (this is often the case). After a while I relented, as he was so insistent. I explained to Catherine that I was just the messenger and gave her his answer. She started laughing, making me think, "Here we go again!" When she managed to control herself, though, she confirmed it, and Hogan gave me a "see, I told you so" look. I was stumped.

She then went on to explain that a few years previously, Hogan had contracted biliary, also known as tick bite fever, and he had to have a blood transfusion to save his life. Just like humans, dogs are needed as blood donors, often to save lives in cases like biliary, surgical procedures, trauma, and accidents. Donor dogs usually go onto a donor roll, and the owner is contacted when the need arises. The donor that gave Hogan blood for his transfusion had been a Labrador. So he had been 100 percent correct in saying that he was part-Labrador, which he thought was the best thing ever. Note to self: Stop thinking and analyzing; just pass the message on!

Hogan, "the Labrador"

CASE STUDY: Justice – The Disappearing Act

Justice was a gorgeous ginger cat who lived in a lovely complex in Durban with Pam and Chris. Chris had cancer and had recently undergone surgery. He was bedridden and slightly depressed, and he took great comfort in Justice lying with him on the bed. Justice would stay with him for a day or two, but then disappear for anything from one to several days. During this time Chris would miss him terribly and it was up to Pam to go out and try to find him.

The complex they lived in was huge, with over 100 units in total, so it really was a major mission to walk around, calling for a missing cat. Pam asked me if I could try to find out where Justice disappeared to, so it would be easier for her to fetch him and bring him back to console Chris. I did the reading at a distance, and Justice knew exactly what was going on in his home. He knew that Chris had cancer and also had a sixth sense that he would soon be losing him. So sometimes it all became a bit much for him, and he took himself off for a break. I asked him where he went, and he said there was no cause for alarm. He mentioned a unit number in the complex, where he went to "recharge."

Justice

When Pam received my email with this information, Justice had once again done a disappearing act for a few days and Chris was asking for him. She was not quite believing what she had read but desperate to find him, she grabbed her cat basket and set off. It was a good walk, 1 km away, and when she eventually arrived at the unit he had mentioned, she stood outside calling his name. Nothing happened at first, then just as she was about to give up, who should come waltzing through the garden with not a care in the world but Justice! More astonished than annoyed she scooped him into the basket and took him back home to reassure Chris.

This pattern of Justice disappearing and Pam going to fetch him continued for several months until Chris was moved to a hospice and finally passed away. The disappearing act was simply a cat trying to deal with the fact that his owner and friend would soon be passing on. Afterwards, he still occasionally disappeared, but Pam always knew where to find him.

CASE STUDY: Boland – Pink not White, Please

Boland is a gorgeous Boerperd who turned out to be a big softie at heart. During the session, the stable manager asked him what they could do for him or if there was anything that he specifically wanted. "Yes, please!" was the answer. "I want marshmallows, but only the pink ones. I don't like the white ones."

This was a strange request from a horse, as how would he even know about marshmallows? He is stabled at a riding school, though, and ridden by children, so my guess was that he had seen someone eating them and fancied one himself. I passed on the request.

A few weeks later, I was back at the yard working with another horse and was happily informed that one of the girls who rides him on a regular basis and absolutely adores him had bought him a packet of marshmallows. Not knowing his color preference, she offered him both pink and white ones after their session. Being a true gentleman, he accepted both colors from her.

After she had gone home, he moved away from the gate post and there, glowing in the Cape sun, were all the white marshmallows, lying in the sand. He had taken the white ones just to make her happy, but spat them out when she wasn't looking.

Boland

9

Animal Communication

So often when doing a reading people ask me if they can also learn how to communicate with animals. The answer is a resounding YES! If I can learn, so can you. That means you can talk to domestic and wild animals, birds, and even insects. You will learn to interact with animals at a deeper, far more fulfilling level than just living together and sharing your life.

We cannot deny that something unseen exists between humans and animals. We know that our animals are sensitive to our emotions—they seem to feel them and react toward them. Now it's time to reverse that process and for you to feel their emotions. How often have you looked at your animal and wondered what they were thinking or wished they could tell you what they want. Now you can find out.

Every thought and feeling you get while in the presence of your animal, especially when you are practicing, will serve as a valuable guide to your intuition, and ultimately, confirm your connection to the animal.

I have included practical exercises of a metaphysical nature in this chapter that will help enhance your intuitive senses. Working through them will help reduce anxiety and stress you might feel and place on yourself as you practice and grow. Once you have the basics and understand how it all works, you can develop your own style of connecting.

Believe in yourself, trust the process, get your mind out of the way and have fun while learning. Let's begin.

There are certain things that need to be acknowledged and accepted before we discuss the steps of connecting to animals.

Love

It is impossible to connect with any form of life if there is no love. In fact, love is the basis of all religions. It is the one thing that connects us to everyone and everything. Essentially, it is completely accepting any person or animal exactly as they are and having no preconceived thoughts, ideas, or judgments about them. In fact, if there is no love and mutual respect for each other, then no communication can take place.

Someone once said, "A dog is the one creature who will love you more than you love yourself." If you understand that and can relate to it, you can place yourself in the dog's, and in fact all animals', so-called shoes. Then the world is yours, and there will be no barriers.

Empathy

Empathy is the experience of understanding another person's condition from their perspective. You place yourself in their shoes and feel what they are feeling—but it is also not allowing yourself to get caught up in the issue at hand. We will deal with this later on, when it comes to emotions. Experience the emotions, but don't hang onto them and make them yours.

Learn to Relax Your Mind

Think of a sponge. That is the perfect visualization of what to expect from your mind when connecting to an animal. Just like a sponge is receptive to any form of water around itself, which it then absorbs and retains, so too must your mind be open to the energy field of an animal when you are in each other's presence.

It is far easier to read and pick up information when you are relaxed and have closed off your mind to outside interferences, such as a radio. How many people, when looking for a place, turn off the radio in their car or the volume down so that they can focus solely on looking for the address or the correct place. The same applies when connecting to an animal.

Telepathy

Telepathy is an ability we all have; we've simply forgotten how to use it. It is a universal language that transcends the boundaries of time, distance, and species. Words are pure energetic language and serve simply as a vehicle for the imagery of our thoughts.

We now know that everything is made up of energy—you, me, trees, plants, animals, and so on. We all have an aura buzzing with energy, and it is this energy we tune in to. You might think you are reading an animal's body language, whereas in fact you are probably communicating with your pets on a higher telepathic plane.

To be receptive to this form of communication, we need to learn to relax. With a certain degree of concentration, each of us is capable of connecting on a telepathic level with an animal we love. Note that telepathy must come from a mutual space of love and respect.

The key to understanding animal communication is that animals think in pictures, and so do we. So to learn to talk to an animal, it's important to have a basic understanding of thought forms, telepathy, and how it works. The idea that our thoughts are powerful is quite scary. In fact, we are all capable of telepathy and have had countless experiences of it.

For example:

- When the phone starts ringing, do you sometimes know who is calling? Have you ever been on your way somewhere and suddenly, without a conscious reason, decided to go a different route, only to discover later that if you had stuck with your original plan you would have been in an accident?

- Have you ever known beyond a shadow of doubt that something is wrong with your child, even though they might be elsewhere, only to find out you were right?

You may have wondered how you knew these things. Was someone telling you? Do you think the images in their brains were in sync with yours? To understand this, we need to acknowledge that we have a sixth sense, the sole purpose of which is to transmit and receive information from other living beings.

The concept of Extra Sensory Perception (ESP) began to be documented at the turn of the century, when scientists started investigating paranormal phenomena. ESP demonstrates the power of the mind and intent. Set the intention and you will connect. As an everyday example of intention, plug in the toaster with the intent to make toast and it will work.

Emotions

In order to learn to communicate with animals, you first need to be aware that they feel emotions just as strongly as we do. Like us, they have a range of emotions, from grief, oversensitivity about how they look, anger, resentment, and jealousy to friendship, compassion, and love. Like us, they have their own issues around people and animal companions or friends. When connecting to an animal, they sometimes pass on the specific emotion to you to help you understand how they feel. Of course, not everyone feels emotions; it depends on how you telepathically pick up information. If you do feel emotions, though, you might find yourself suddenly getting extremely emotional and shedding a tear as you get the image of how they feel about a friend or loved one.

You may even be overcome by grief or loss after the passing of a friend. To feel these emotions is perfectly fine for the session, but try to remain objective and not take on too much; you need to protect yourself.

If you don't follow this process, you might find yourself carrying around a particular emotion for days afterwards, not really understanding why you are feeling like you do, until you remember you did a session and are dealing with someone else's emotions and issues.

Meditation

The easiest way to learn to connect with animals is by learning how to meditate, so that you can teach your mind to slow down and listen. Meditation gives you more time by making your mind calmer and more focused. It helps you overcome stress and find inner peace and balance.

When I first started meditating, many years ago, I was extremely nervous. It took me a few weeks of constant practice to find out what works for me and how my mind works. To give you an example: I always keep a pen and paper nearby when I meditate. As soon as I try to relax, it's as though my mind fights it, and I come up with lists of things that I need to do or buy at the shops. So now I just write down everything that comes up in the first few minutes, and once that is done my mind is open and clear.

I also listen to music for meditation and relaxation, such as the recorded sounds of the sea or the forest. There are hundreds of CDs of such music to choose from. To this day, if I am out somewhere and hear an old favorite tune, my mind immediately slows down and I become more relaxed as I resonate with it and go into "the zone." It also helps before an event, when I find myself particularly nervous, such as public speaking. I listen to the music or try to hum the tune in order to relax myself. You need to establish your own pattern of behavior or ritual around meditation.

Meditation Exercise

There are many different ways of meditating, and you need to discover what is right for you. In the following meditation, I am briefly going to cover the steps for the best known technique.

- Wait until things at home are quiet and relaxed, then put yourself into a comfortable sitting position and close your eyes. Rest your hands in your lap.

- Become aware of your breathing, follow it, and try to breathe slowly and deeply. Breathe in, and hold the breath for a count of five, then breathe out. Your attention will be on your breath, and this will relax your mind. Now imagine all your anxiety and tension leaving your body and draining out through your feet.

- Once you are feeling more relaxed, imagine yourself being in a beautiful setting in nature. It could be anywhere you want, somewhere where you find comfort—a waterfall, a stream, on top of a mountain, in a forest, or by the sea. Whichever place you choose needs to be near a body of water, as water is used in the physical and the spiritual sense to cleanse ourselves.

- Take some time to visualize everything you find comfort in, and add things you like and find serene. Take note of the colors, textures, and shapes of the space you are creating.

- This is your place that you are creating and visualizing and may return to at any stage you wish.

- Now you need to ground yourself. This helps you avoid becoming light-headed and experiencing what some people call a "floaty feeling." It also helps you to relax and focus and come back to reality at the end of a session.

- Imagine yourself as a tree. As you are sitting quietly, see yourself grow roots from the base of your spine. The roots penetrate through the chair you are sitting on, carry on growing through the floor, and deep down into the earth. You may imagine it to be like the root of a strong tree. This root searches down through all the different layers of the earth until it reaches the center of the earth and wraps itself around the core. Become aware of the red, pulsating energy of this core. Guide its progress, absorbing it, as it flows back up through the roots and into the base of your spine. It travels up your spinal column and out through the top of your head.

- Continue to draw this energy upward, becoming aware of and connecting to cosmic energy. This means you are now grounded and connected to base energy. You are also now ready to start the process of connecting with an animal.

Visualization

How often have you had a conversation with someone and perhaps initially couldn't grasp what the person was trying to say? Then suddenly, in your mind's eye, you had a flash of insight or a picture popped in that clarified it. Once you have the image you immediately understood.

As humans working with animals, we need to use words only until we have transferred an image from our mind to their mind. From their side, they commonly transfer images straight to our mind.

Having a good imagination and being able to visualize is extremely useful in animal communication as you need to be able to show an animal by using visualization what their owner wants them to do. An example is when a cat or a dog has developed the tendency to go to the bathroom in the house and not go outside. If there is no physical or emotional issue that needs to be tackled, then you need to show that animal where the owner wants them to urinate. Sometimes this is something that needs a little negotiating as the animal does not like what is being offered so a treat system or a pee pad (in the case of older animals who cannot always hold it in) needs to be discussed.

The Power of Imagination

Visualization is the process of forming an image in the mind, which is more than a picture as it can include feelings and senses.

Read aloud the following to help you along:

- The lovely cat was walking on the wall, tail in the air as if it didn't have a care in the world.

- Spotting something on the ground, the cat slowed and cautiously sat, its tail swinging mischievously back and forth. Slowly it crouched forward and went into a stalking position…

Think about what you saw in your mind's eye when you were reading that. Did it play in your mind as if you were watching a movie? Were there any features of the cat that stood out? For example, what was the color of its eyes, and was it a he or a she? Did you notice the type of tree branch, or what the wall looked like? If you did, you are on the right track. That is how you should convey images to an animal.

When our brains are in a relaxed state, taking us into a meditative space, visualization helps us to see images not only from our own mind's eye but also from another's. When talking to others or thinking to ourselves, we hold in our mind a series of pictures, sometimes with very strong emotions associated with them. Yet we tend to think that verbal communication is the only way we can communicate. How wrong we are!

When we form an image in the mind, the power of imagination is utilized. This is the basic creative energy of everything around us and of the universe itself. When we visualize, we literally create a screen in our minds, and with our eyes closed (or sometimes open), play a movie of our choice upon that screen.

Visualization assists the brain in developing the skills of observing detail and focusing the mind. This all contributes to you being able to connect telepathically to an animal.

Animal Connection Exercises

When you begin to connect with animals, it's normal to be nervous. As a starting point, work with animals you don't know. To this day, when someone phones me to book a consultation and they want to tell me what is going on, I immediately stop them. I want to go into a session and be able to pick up what is going on. The more you know about an animal, the harder it is, as you already have so much information and it might add to the feeling of pressure. Knowing nothing helps a great deal, as you have no preconceived ideas and your mind will then be a blank canvas. That is the best space to be in as your intuition will then need to kick in and your telepathy muscle will get some exercise.

Connection Meditation

This is a meditation you can use to connect with any animal, whether they are present or in a photograph (be sure you can see the animal's eyes).

- Find a quiet and comfortable space. Relax your body from head to toe. Become aware of your breathing, and consciously breathe deeply, inhaling and exhaling.

- In your mind's eye (or the movie screen we call our mind), go through the meditation preparation technique of visualization and grounding. Set the intention of connecting to the animal in question by having a photograph at hand. Visualize your heart chakra opening, or a heart with a lid on it that opens.

- Then visualize a beautiful pink bridge of love extending from your heart and flowing straight to the animal/insect/plant's heart. You can also visualize yourself as a sponge, simply absorbing their energy. See this bridge connecting your heart and the animal's heart.

- Pay attention to whatever you experience, but do not overthink it or your mind may get in the way.

- Make notes and ask questions, if necessary.

- When you have finished with the communication, thank the animal for its time.

- Imagine your heart chakra closing to a point where you feel comfortable.

- Slowly bring yourself back to the present by focusing on your physical body, your breath, and your physical surroundings, and when you are ready, gently open your eyes.

Types of Telepathy

The next step in the process is determining how you picked up this information. Over the years of teaching workshops, I have come to understand that when it comes to animal communication there are different kinds of telepathy. Knowing *how* you receive information allows you to validate that you are connecting, so you will be less likely to dismiss information when it comes to you.

Mental Telepathists

These are people who tend to feel deeply, but do not necessarily express these feelings in the physical through emotional release. They often receive information in images.

Emotional Telepathists

These are people who seem to feel and release on a physical level. They might get emotional or even cry. This is simply part of the process, and if this is you, don't try to hold back your tears. The tears serve as confirmation that you have connected and can now carry on with the session. Emotional telepathists often receive information via an emotion or a gut feeling.

Which One Are You?

How are you experiencing the connection:

- Do you feel it in your heart?

- Do you get a gut feeling or even feel slightly nauseous?

- Do you see an image in your mind and/or just know something?

- Does it tingle anywhere?

It's useful to document your sessions so that when you look back, you can start to pick up a pattern.

Points to Note

- Make sure you always do the meditation preparation technique before attempting to connect.

- Sometimes you may experience suddenly knowing something, when no rational thought could validate how you came to that conclusion. The mind can then rebel against the information. If this happens to you and you start to doubt yourself, don't.

- Understand the energy of what you are trying to convey.

- When receiving mental images, try not to overanalyze them. Just accept them as they come.

- Realize that under intense emotional conditions, such as love or grief, your awareness is heightened.

- When you do start to pick up the animal "calls," you may notice not only a telepathic transference of pictures from their minds to yours, and vice versa, but also that you can pick up on the animal's emotions and feel physical sensations in your body that an animal is experiencing. You might even get images of their favorite food or even taste the food (which is not always pleasant, especially if they do not like their food).

- Be aware of any emotions you have during a communication experience. Sometimes it is easier to feel an animal's emotions than rely on them telling you.

- The same applies to physical sensations. If you suspect they might be feeling unwell, then ask them to show you on your body where they're hurting. Be prepared to feel discomfort, even pain, in your body. Once you have confirmed it, ask them to remove it.

Telepathy Exercise

This exercise is a way to prove to yourself that you can communicate on a telepathic level with an animal. When attempting the exercise, make sure the animal is calm and relaxed. If they are otherwise preoccupied—for example, busy digging a hole or barking at the postman—they will be distracted and won't pay attention to anything telepathic.

1. Sit quietly, and close your eyes.

2. Do the preparation technique of visualization and grounding.

3. Set the intention of communicating with your animal.

4. Now, if you have a dog, envision yourself getting up and walking to where you keep the dog's leash, taking it off the hook. In your heart, feel the excitement of the walk and the intended route you want to follow. Also envision any landmarks you may see along the way.

5. If you have a cat, follow the same directions, only envision yourself in the kitchen or wherever you feed your animal. See yourself opening a tin of tuna or their favorite meal. As you open it, smell it and try to capture the taste of the food and how good it will be to eat.

6. Now open your eyes and see if you have any response from your animal. Is your dog looking at you with the excitement of a promised walk? Is your cat hungrily rubbing against your leg?

NOTE: If your animal responded to the above, it is only fair to offer what you promised, either a walk for the dog or some food for the cat, and a big smile from you!

Actual Communication

First, let's establish why we would want to talk to animals. People all have their own reasons, but essentially, it can help to answer a lot of important questions, not only for you but for the animal, too. It also raises your awareness of all animals collectively. We need to learn to honor all creatures, no matter how insignificant they seem to us.

We are all here for a reason. So what exactly is meant by animal communication or interspecies communication?

Animal communication is talking to an animal using telepathy, psychokinetic energy, or extrasensory perception (ESP). We may receive images, feelings, sounds, or sensations from them.

There are many reasons this can happen:

• Having unconditional love for the animal, or coming from a place of love.

• Having the intention and wanting to connect (one of the Laws of Nature is that energy follows thought: Believe it, trust that it can happen, and it will).

• Being receptive and fully in the now.

• Respecting the individual character of the animal, as they are all unique.

• Picking up their energy field, whether intentionally or not.

Animals communicate with pictures or feelings that they transmit telepathically. They are sensitive, intuitive, and intelligent, and they love and care for each other and for you. Pets are very much like humans in their feelings and emotions, which makes them sensitive to human emotions. For example, if the owner is depressed, they feel the unhappiness, and vice versa. They understand all the problems within their home, and all they want is love and security.

They never forget when someone has hurt them or shown them kindness. If there is a change in their behavior, there is always a good reason for it. Often the problem has originated with the owner and not the animal.

Sometimes animals have a hard time understanding the complexities of human behavior, as we sometimes battle to understand our own behavior and that of others. In fact, human behavior is often far worse and more unpredictable than animal behavior. We simply need to look at our planet, and what we humans have done to it, to see this. Animals will never deliberately hurt anyone without good reason.

They are like children, in that they crave our attention and affection. When they feel they are being ignored, they find ways to get our attention. Animals don't really care about the type of attention they are getting, or whether it's positive or negative. Generally speaking, the greater the lack of attention, the worse their behavior becomes.

How the Communication Happens

It is not necessary to know an animal before you try to connect with it. You and the animal can be hundreds of miles apart, never having met or spoken before. All it takes is the intention to connect, a photo of the animal, and its name and location.

Some cultures, such as the Masai in Kenya, believe that if you take a photo of a person, the picture will then contain the soul or the essence of that person. Many tourists are ignorant of this or lack the manners to ask if they mind, and the Masai have been known to get very upset if photographed without prior consent. It has nothing to do with payment or money; it is a belief system and a valid one.

When a photograph is taken, it captures the energy field of the subject being shot, not visible to the eye but obviously visible to the camera. The energetic fingerprints of all the people who are in the picture are then on film. With photography, the film remains invisible until it has been developed, and those energetic effects also remain impalpable until the developing process has been applied. We can then pick up information from the photograph.

Wherever there is energy, there is information, and we can tune into pictures and other objects, too, even the chair we are sitting on. This is also known as psychometry (gaining information by holding or touching an object).

The Science Behind It

Humans have always wanted to understand the world and how it works in a better way than whatever era they find themselves living in. The more advanced we become, the more we seem to enjoy the challenge of finding out more. It's who and what we are.

J.J. Thomson was a physicist who is credited for discovery of the atom, way back in 1987. The earth, our bodies, the plants around us, the couch you are sitting on, and everything around us is made up of atoms. Atoms all contain exactly the same particle, just in varying amounts. Due to the density of everyday things, such as a chair, we cannot see each individual atom; we would like to, but the human eye is incapable of such scrutiny. What we *are* able to see is the finished product—the complete human body, the table, the chair, and everything around us. If no one ever told you that your body is made up of atoms or is a perfect electrical circuit, you would not know any better. Logically, our body is made up of blood, skin, tissue, and a skeletal system, so why on earth would we think it was made up of something else? Because we have always wanted to explore and understand the science behind things and the universe.

We now accept that our bodies are made up of atoms; science tells us that. All atoms contain electromagnetic energy, which is invisible to the human eye. The simplest way to understand this concept is to make a bowl of Jello and use it as an analogy. When the Jello has been made and poured into a bowl, simply add a slice of fruit or two.

Pop it into the fridge, as you normally would. When it's set, imagine yourself as a piece of fruit inside the bowl. If there is more than one piece of fruit, imagine it as a friend or an animal. The Jello all around you is matter or electromagnetic energy. Moving the bowl causes the pieces of fruit to wobble in unison with the jelly. If you were to insert a spoon into the Jello to get the fruit out, it would affect the whole structure of the Jello, and the spoon will leave its mark, even after taking it out.

Now eat the Jello—all of it. Before you wash the bowl, notice how tiny bits of Jello stick to the sides of the bowl, even though there is nothing left to eat. So, although the Jello has been eaten, there are still little bits remaining, like little pieces of energy. The Jello you ate was also made up of those little pieces of Jello, or those pieces of energy. You and the Jello are now one; you are not separate in any way, just like all living creatures are not separate in any way.

With the advancement of quantum physics, there is now enough scientific evidence to prove the existence of the human energy field. Humans have an energy field, which we term an "aura." We can now even take photos of our aura, or that of plants or animals, using the latest technology. In a previous chapter, we have covered how this energy moves when we are connecting with animals.

If energy is all around us, everything that we see and touch is then made up of energy, and it flows through us and is changed by us. Based on this knowledge, we are all energetically in tune and connected with the world around us. If we are surrounded by electromagnetic energy, could that then be perceived as thought?

The concept of a zero-point energy field is the theory that all living creatures are able to communicate with each other due to the law of nature, also called resogenesis. We all are part of one big organism, including Earth and the entire universe. Based on this theory, it is possible to communicate with each and every living thing.

We are generally taught that if we cannot explain a thing logically, then we should ignore or dismiss it. Logic is based on the five senses, and we are only now starting to use our sixth sense and begin to understand it. Animals, insects, plants, and humans are all made up of atoms, as we have discussed; we all have electromagnetic energy. Can we then agree that we are all connected, and that our actions and thoughts all affect each other?

Your Energy Field

The following is an exercise to help you to see your energy. This will help you understand and explore your own energy field, thereby becoming more open to seeing and feeling that of an animal. When you start seeing and feeling it, it becomes tangible and you have confirmation that it exists. It also demonstrates that we don't actually have to be touching something to feel it, as everything is energetically connected. We are living in one big hologram.

You can do this exercise anywhere. The only rule is to be relaxed and try to have a neutral wall (beige or white) or tile near you. The bath is my favorite place, as you are feeling warm and relaxed.

Exercise

- Place a chair in front of a wall and sit down.

- Breathe deeply and feel yourself relaxing. You have no expectations; you are just playing.

- Now hold up both your hands in front of you, with the thumbs nearly touching. Find the center of your hands—your thumbs— and focus on them. After a few seconds, it may feel like your eyes are going a bit fuzzy or bleary. That is normal. Allow it to happen. Don't try to control your eyes by rubbing them and bringing them back into focus.

- Focusing on your thumbs, extend your vision so that you see both of your hands. Now slowly draw your eyes back to focus on your thumbs again, then back out again to include both of your hands. What you are trying to do is soft-focus your eyes, so you can see the energy of your hands. At first it will look like a shadow, then after a few attempts, you may see a very light blue or yellow color.

- Once you have seen your energy field, try the exercise again but move your hands so that your finger tips are slightly touching, then move them apart, and watch the energy flow from your fingers. You should notice that the energy around your fingers is connected, even though your fingers and hands are apart. It might take a few attempts to learn to soft-focus your eyes before you see anything; persistence pays off.

You can also try this exercise when out in nature. Find a tree, and look at the top. Soft-focus your eyes so you can see the haze around the tree. With patience and practice, this is an excellent way of teaching yourself to see plant auras and the energy field. When I first started playing around with this exercise, it took around three weeks for me to finally see the aura of a plant, and it was so spectacular it was something I shall never forget and so worth the effort.

Sensing an Animal's Field

Now you have seen your field, it is time to try and feel the field of an animal. Try doing this exercise with a variety of different animals, if you can, and see if you can feel a difference. With animals, it is easier to feel the field before you start seeing it with the naked eye. If you feel it, you will believe it, which is one step closer to talking to an animal.

If you have a domestic animal who sits on you or close to you when you relax, use the opportunity to do this exercise. For bigger animals, such as horses, sheep, or cows, you will need to go out into the yard to find them. Ask someone to help you with a rope or a halter. Just remember (especially with sheep and cows) that they might move away in the beginning, and that's normal. It's also not a good idea to scan the physical body in a herd environment. Ideally, try this in a stable or paddock when they are on their own. There is sometimes too much jostling taking place in a herd, and they will be aware of it and want to respond. Just persist, using love and patience, and they will feel the shift and become more relaxed.

- Take a deep breath, and try to relax, bringing yourself to the present. Then stretch out your hand to above their body (about 5 cm away from the surface of the body). There is no need to physically touch them, but it can reassure them. I am right-handed, so I touch the animal with my left hand to reassure them and scan with my right hand just above the body. You can scan by touching the body all over, but just as we have private places on our bodies, animals do, too, and we need to respect that.

- Now, slowly move your hand up and down the length of the body, start at the head, move over the neck, shoulders, down the front legs, the stomach, kidneys, back legs, and then the tail, if it has one. Then move to the other side of the body, and scan there. It helps to study animal anatomy so that you know where all the organs are situated.

- Pay attention to what you experience. Remember that in this exercise you are using your intuition and your sixth sense. Do you sense anything? Think of your other five senses and notice whatever comes into your mind? Don't discard anything, and also be aware of any aches and pains in your body before you start.

The reason for that is that sometimes an animal will transfer a feeling of being unwell on a certain area of your body.

- When that happens step away and let the feeling pass, then go back to the area of the body where you first sensed it and see if it comes back.

- Do you feel anything like warmth/cold? Is it all over the body or just in a certain area?

- Does the animal move in any way when you do this?

- Does the animal stand still?

- Does the animal seem sensitive or move slightly away in any area, such as shifting from leg to leg, moving away from you, sighing, and so on?

- You might become aware of a smell, taste, or sound, or even sense something. Anything and everything is important, so don't discard anything.

- The animal's reaction to what you are doing will be your greatest confirmation. There is no right and wrong – the experience is different for all of us.

Questioning Techniques

These pointers will help you to work with questions in a constructive way:

- Ask only one question at a time, then pause and wait for an answer.
- Ask open questions instead of closed (yes/no) questions. For example, instead of asking "Don't you like your food?" ask something like "How do you feel about your food?" When asking a question about food, don't be surprised if they put the taste of it in your mouth.
- Avoid the word "why" and any undertones of accusation. Rather, ask, "What makes you...?"
- Keep it simple; just be open and listen.

- If you are struggling, try visualizing the question floating toward the animal and the answers coming back to you like bubbles, or even yourself as a sponge, absorbing the animal's energy.

- Before ending the communication, ask the animal if there is anything else they would like to share.

Following you find some suggestions for questions that you could ask the animal when you connect.

Horse

- How do you feel about your food?

- Is there anything you don't like (be aware they might give you pictures of it), e.g. a supplement?

- Is there anything else you would like in your food? (The answer is negotiable, not always a given, as it must be discussed with the owner and sometimes they ask for things they know they should not have.).

- How do you enjoy your paddock, outrides? Is there anything you would change?

- How does the saddle feel on your back? Is it comfortable? Anywhere that is too tight?

- How does the girth feel? (Be aware of your stomach.)

- How does the bridle and bit feel? Is it uncomfortable or pinching? Where? (Be aware of your mouth.)

- If in a herd – is there any one you connect with?

- If in a paddock – how do you feel about your paddock friend? (They might not like the other horse at all and would like a change. If they want a change, then discuss with whom, and see if it's possible. This is important to horses.)

- Do you have any pain or discomfort? (Go through the entire body, from nose to tail.)

- How do you feel about the farrier? Does he do a good job?

- When the chiropractor returns, is there any particular area you would like them to work on?

- Do you have a best friend?
- Are you lonely?
- What is your favorite activity?
- How do you feel about your horse trailer?
- Do you like to go to horse shows?

Dog

A very important subject – FOOD

- Do you enjoy your food? (If the answer is not really, try to get more information. Does it not taste good? Wrong brand? Want something totally different?)
- Are you bored with the food?
- Does your food fill you up?
- What is your favorite outing, and why?
- How do you feel about your bed?
- If you don't like it, what can you suggest to change things?
- Do you have a favorite toy?
- Show me your best friend.
- Are you sore anywhere on your body?
- What is your favorite color?
- Is there any game you really enjoy?

Cat

- Where do you like to be petted the most—head/back/ears?
- What would you like to change about your household?
- How do you feel about the other animal in your house?
- If you could change anything what would it be?
- Do you get enough stimulation?
- How far do you wander at night (if they do) and go visit?
- How do you feel about your food?

- Is there any colored (food) tin you enjoy more than the other?
- Is there anything about the routine you share with your human that has changed?
- Where is your favorite place to sleep? Why?
- Do you go for takeout at the neighbors? (If yes) what do they feed you? (If you don't like what you hear, negotiate to change the food so they don't go eat somewhere else.)

When you have asked a question and you get a positive response expand on that. One question leads to another, and without realizing it, you will be chatting away with perfect ease.

Problems with Connecting

There are a few things that can get in the way when trying to connect with an animal:

- Your mind discarding everything you feel.
- If you're experiencing insecurity and self-doubt, do some deep breathing and restate your intention to connect.
- When your mental chatter gets in the way, try locking your thoughts away, or see yourself writing them on a blackboard and then rubbing them off.
- If you're nervous about the responsibility of connecting, try to hold a perspective of compassionate nonattachment to the outcome. Do what you can to be of service, then release your connection.
- If you're worried about interpretations and drawing conclusions, be aware that you have the option to choose to ignore what you've picked up and simply accept things as they are. You are not doing this to judge; you serve as an intermediary between the animal and the owner.
- If you're worried that what you're picking up is just your imagination or a projection, ask the animal to confirm.
- Maintain healthy boundaries by protecting your physical, emotional, and mental bodies in a silver bubble of protection.

Stages of Development

As you develop and hone this new skill, it helps to become aware of what is going on within yourself. The more you do this, the more you will learn to trust yourself, and your confidence will grow.

Especially at the beginning, many people discount the information they get, due to uncertainty. Try not to discount anything. Make a note of your connections, including what you felt and experienced within yourself, and the information you receive about the animal concerned. In time, you will see a pattern start to emerge. This works in different ways for everyone, so the trick is to recognize how it works for you. As you progress, your sense of knowing will increase in leaps and bounds. You may find yourself picking up information about yourself and other people, as well as about animals. It is up to you to listen and use it wisely.

Also, the more you practice, the more your vibration changes and strengthens and the more animals will be drawn to you. The first sign of this vibration change is that animals, both domestic and wild, will seek you out in preference to other people. When this happens, just be in the moment and enjoy it for what it is—a connection and a sign of just how much your intuition is growing.

I recently had a huge cockroach follow me around like a dog for two nights and sleep under my bed, simply because he battled with anxiety due to the rains that were expected and he did not have enough confidence in himself to choose an area where he felt safe. On the morning of the third day he had disappeared, problem over. So also be open to the fact that they may ask you to do something or help, and you might feel an overwhelming urge to fulfill that request, as weird as it may seem.

Questioning and conversation will flow much more easily, and instead of just asking questions and waiting for answers, you will find yourself listening a lot more. They will tell you what's important to them, about their lives and their friends, toys they play with, or what is happening at home. The more you listen from a place of nonjudgment, the stronger the connection and trust between you will grow.

You may eventually begin to have everyday conversations without thinking about it. For example, perhaps you're unpacking the groceries and your cat comes over to sniff something in particular, or you're in the garden, with a conversation going on in your mind, and then only later realize what was going on. It's a wonderful and special process; enjoy every minute.

Ways to Practice at Home

Psychometry is the ability to discover facts about an event or person by touching inanimate objects associated with them, such as photographs. The objective of this exercise is to see if you can pick up information from photographs of animals.

You can use photographs or hair cut with the owner's permission, or ask the owner for a small piece of hair (not the half a piece of mane I received the other day), a favorite toy, collar, or blanket—anything that the animal has been in contact with for a while. If you are working with an object, the longer it has belonged to the animal, the more of that animal's energy will be on it and the more tangible it will be to pick up information.

Practicing this helps to exercise the neurons in your brain, so that you are learning and developing not only the telepathic part of your brain but also your intuitive side.

Have the object or photograph near you. Meditate and get into a relaxed state, and hold the object or photograph in your hand. If working with an object, close your eyes and become aware of any sensation in your body. Do you feel happy or sad? Is there a particular type of emotion you are feeling? Start off like that, keeping an open mind, and just let things come in.

If you are working with a photograph, you can look at the picture, follow the animal connection guideline, and proceed as you would if you were getting information from an animal who is with you.

An advanced way of practicing psychometry is to get several photographs together and place them in envelopes so that you cannot see the pictures, then read them like that. You are forced to rely on your sixth sense, on the information you are getting, and not let your mind get in the way—a difficult exercise but fun, anyway.

Note: This is an incredibly difficult exercise, and few people get very accurate answers in the beginning. Only with practice will your score improve.

General Advice and Tips

A few general tips for when you start to communicate:

- If you feel particularly "floaty," emotional, or ungrounded after a connection, drink a glass of water or eat something to help ground yourself.

- Be patient and persistent in trying to communicate. Remind yourself that Rome was not built in a day and developing this skill takes time and plenty of practice.

- Try not to eat a big meal for at least two hours before a session as it slows down your energy. It's highly unlikely that you will get hungry during the session, anyway. Because you are working with energy, your body is being replenished automatically by the interaction. Sometime afterwards, you may remember that you haven't eaten in a while, at which time go ahead and do so.

- Sometimes, you may feel very emotional after a particular connection or tracking attempt, and that feeling can remain for several days afterwards. Be aware of it, and send healing to the animal and to your own emotional body.

- The more you practice, the easier it becomes to handle your emotions. Having said that, sometimes emotions do stick with you, no matter what you do. We are human after all.

Working with Different Animals

When you start working with your new skill, try and visit some of the owners and animals and work face to face. You can also work at a distance via your computer or photographs, but people do like to meet and build a rapport with you.

Although doing this work can be emotional, it can also become one of the most rewarding careers there are, especially as you begin to build those relationships.

More Tips and Guidelines

When you start connecting to animals, it opens up a world you have never imagined. The more you practice on a variety of different animals the easier things will be and the better you will become. The following tips will assist you in working with animals that you may not be familiar with. Some people are not that practical so I am really covering all aspects in the list.

- Skirts are fine for cats and dogs but not horses. High heels are best left in your closet; jeans, comfortable shoes, and a good dose of humor are better suited to an animal communication session.

- Try not to connect with an animal around feeding time. The animal may be so focused on not being fed that making a connection could be difficult. If it's not your animal, ask the owner to feed the animal half an hour before you get there to avoid any unnecessary anxiety around food.

- Be aware of your own meal times, and make allowances for it or your mind may be very aware that you are hungry, which can make it harder to connect. As you progress, you may find that you don't become hungry until at least an hour after a connection has finished, and then you are starving.

- Be aware that occasionally an emotional release can cause the animal to become slightly irritated. Swinging of the head, slight anxiety or discomfort are all signs of this. If this does happen, it doesn't mean you have done anything wrong. Simply stay calm and send some light pink and blue light around the animal, holding the animal in that space until they have worked through the emotion they are experiencing. It's unlikely to last longer than five minutes at most and you may notice an almost tangible release afterwards. Some animals sigh, some grow quiet and others might retreat and lie down somewhere. Let this serve as validation for you that something huge has shifted for the animal and allowed healing to take place.

- If it is not your own animal, ask the owner before a session to make a list of questions (within reason) that they would like to ask the animal. In general, try to limit the number of questions to 10 for cats, dogs, and small domesticated animals. Horse owners will often have more questions, due to the nature and complexity of horses and the associated sport. If you start the session by connecting and allowing general information to come through, very often many of their questions have been answered before you get to the Q&A.

- While you are practicing and building up your confidence, if an owner asks if they can invite a few friends to watch, it is perfectly okay to turn them down. People are naturally inquisitive, and if they interfere or ask questions, it can become difficult, as well as putting extra pressure on you. Feel free to tell the owner you need to work in silence and only deal with them and their animal. Also, extremely sensitive and personal information sometimes comes out, and it is difficult and unprofessional to relay that type of information in front of other people, potentially putting people on the spot when it's unnecessary. Use your discretion, and keep your boundaries firm.

Tips for Working with Dogs

Ask the owners to allow you to work where the animal feels comfortable—the kennel outside is generally not a good idea for either of you. If you prefer sitting on the ground with the animal, ask for a pillow or take one with you to avoid potential discomfort.

When arriving at the house, greet the owner first and ignore the dog. If the dog jumps up, gently place your hand on top of its head, and tell it (and show it) to keep its paws on the ground. Dogs are pack animals, and if you immediately greet the dog like a long-lost friend, he will consider you beneath him in the pack. That's an especially bad idea if you are dealing with a behavioral problem.

Avoid eye contact with the dog to begin with, too. In dog language, direct eye contact is considered a challenge, which you want to avoid, especially when dealing with a huge Boerbul or Rottweiler. For the most part, the minute you walk into the home, they will feel your energy and know that you are there for their good, but there are occasional exceptions. Following the right pattern of behavior from the start helps prevent problems down the line.

Tips for Working with Cats

Ask the owner to get the cat inside a room, with closed doors and windows, before you arrive. If that's not possible, ask them to catch the cat while you close the windows, doors, and other access points—cats are escape artists, and the last thing you want is to have to run from room to room, trying to connect with the cat (owners don't understand this; they think it's highly amusing to watch and rarely help).

With cats, you need to build a sense of trust at the start; it's all about will and power. You need to prove yourself to them. Once you have done this, they settle down, relax, and the conversation flows.

Cats almost always have a dry sense of humor. You may also be shocked to learn that they sometimes lie, which they find extremely entertaining. Again, it's about trust and us taking things too seriously. If it happens, share the joke and try to get them back to focusing and interacting.

Tips for Working with Horses

Wear the correct clothing and shoes. A hoof on your toes will not be a pleasant experience if you are wearing flip flops! Dress appropriately, in old clothes that can get covered in hair and hay. If possible, ask the owner to put the horse in the stable for the period of the session in advance of your arrival. Also be aware of the timing of the appointment, and try to avoid late afternoons. It is extremely difficult, not to mention unfair on the horse, to try and hold their attention when there is a sudden burst of curiosity at who is being led in and/or being fed. They also get hungry, and if they are waiting for their food, you are going to get an extremely irritated, hungry, and grumpy horse that feels you are withholding his food from him. Respect feeding times, and work around them.

If you are not used to horses and are dealing with a temperamental one, stand outside the stable until you have done a few sessions and feel easier around them. If you're standing close by, be aware that horses may kick or swing around suddenly at a sound in the yard and step on your toe. If they do either of these things, your ability to concentrate is likely to be extremely difficult for the rest of the session!

Also watch out for car keys hanging from your pockets and sunglasses on top of your head. Horses love sparkly things and will quickly grab them if given the opportunity and they are in the mood. If they do, get the item back, and laugh it off.

Tips for Working with Rats and Hamsters

You can work with rats or hamsters either on a bed, or allow them to move over you, if you're okay with that. Lizards can remain in their cages. Rats and hamsters enjoy exploring but are nocturnal, so it is wise to try and read them at night, not during the day when they are trying to sleep. Do not attempt this if you are at all squeamish, especially as they might urinate on you as part of the process.

Also bear in mind that some lizards, like the bearded lizard, tend to flare up if they get anxious. Don't be intimidated, just try to remain calm, acknowledge that they have been heard, and carry on.

Animal Humor and Comments

So you complain about your dog's farts, do you? Be aware that hell hath no fury like a dog who has been blamed for his owner's farts. They don't get mad; they get even. You have been warned!

If you bake a lot and spread the results of your efforts out on the kitchen counter to cool down, please note that your cat may not be applauding you for your marvelous creations. Instead, they will be complaining that you are hogging all the counterspace! ("Leave some space for me please, Mom!")

A horse will sometimes tell their owner to please go out and treat themselves to a new pair of riding boots—no more takkies (trainers/running shoes). ("You ride like a professional, so dress like one. Buy things for me, but please spoil yourself, too!")

A message from your cats and dogs: "Do not complain about my breath after feeding me fish or a smelly bone! Man, you should seriously smell your breath first thing in the morning, but I kiss you good morning anyway!"

"So you tell me my bum is getting bigger, do you? I know you're joking, but just remember this bum needs to accommodate an even bigger bum that gets into the saddle!" (And then you get the smiley face.)

For a horse, there is no other creature as weird as an ostrich.

If an animal tells you to fix your car, please do it. A vehicle brings you to them, and they identify you with your car, so they do listen to it and know when something is not right. If anything goes wrong with the car, it takes you away from them, and they don't want that to happen.

When we ask a direct question of an animal, we don't always get a straightforward answer; sometimes things come out in a roundabout way. Also, what seems direct to us can be complicated or illogical to them. For example, asking "Are you sleeping in your shelter at night?" they might give you (1) "Well, actually, someone else is taking my spot, and I don't want to cause any problems by telling you that", or (2) the horse may roll their eyes and says "YESSSSS - and if you got here early enough, you would see I am covered in shavings," followed by a big sigh (This should be obvious. Why are you asking?).

Domesticated animals have learned that if you purse your lips at them and say give me a kiss and they do it back to you, that makes you very happy, and they will do anything to make you happy. Please don't compare them to a cow or tell them they look like one. Cows are not the only animals with spots. It's a major insult, and they often bring it up in a reading. They are unique and proud of their spots.

If the family goes on a banting (no sugar diet), do not cheat. If you walk through the door with sugar on your breath from the fudge you sneakily ate in the car and did not share with the dog, your dog will not think twice about calling you out on it in a session with your husband present (especially if you've been constantly nagging him not to cheat on his diet).

If you own a rat and want to do something special for them, put up a display of Christmas lights at night. They absolutely love them.

If you live in an apartment block, your animals know what the upstairs neighbors cook. Most animals hate the smell of cabbage, especially if they are not used to it.

If you are OCD about shoes, your animals won't understand why your shoes have to be lined up in your cupboard. They will still love you for it, though.

Even though your rescue dog came from another part of town and you live in a more affluent neighborhood, they still keep the dialect of the area they are from. When spoken by a dog or a cat in an exclusive residential area in Cape Town, the Cape dialect can be very entertaining. Caring is sharing. That applies to food and to 99 percent of the dogs in our lives. Especially to bassett hounds who if they don't get to share will leave a stinky present for you in an obvious place to show their displeasure.

Molly

Horses don't particularly enjoy human food, but they can smell it on you. When they ask why their beloved human eats white worms (spaghetti) or their breath smells fishy and like the sea (sushi), it makes a reading very entertaining.

It's essential to negotiate with dogs when you want to change a routine in the household, such as them waking you up at 5 a.m. for a cuddle. Set a time that would work better for you (within reason), such as 6 a.m., and when the dog keeps their end of the deal, reward them with a treat and acknowledgment. If not, be prepared to be woken earlier than usual.

Conclusion

A sincere thank you to all my clients and even more importantly, to their animals, who have contributed to this book. You make my life whole and complete. If it weren't for each and every one of you sharing your lives, stories, and healing with me, this book could not have happened in the way it did.

Every time I connect with an animal, I learn a little more about them and the world we live in. On a personal level, too, I have learned so much from studying this subject and doing this work, and my life has moved forward in leaps and bounds. Even during the process of writing this book, my personal levels of understanding and consciousness have shifted dramatically.

To all the animal lovers out there, I hope this book helps to change the way that you look at, think about, and interact with animals, both tame and wild. May it change your life, too, and bring you closer to your own animals.

Illustrations and Case Studies

List of Illustrations

Illustration Credits

The author acknowledges with thanks the copyright for the following photos and illustrations used in this book:

p. 33 – Santa © Trudi Gill
p. 40 – Sebastian © Maryse Pennington Collins
p. 45 – Fabio © Heidi Stumpf
p. 56 – Rafiki © Lynn Haupt
p. 68 – Figure 31 © Damian Keenan
p. 72 – Figure 33 ©Tammy Mustoe
p. 90 – Burning Bright © Tracy Robertson
p. 104 – King © Bernadette de Kock
p. 107 – Figure 51 © Kaabsregel / Dreamstime.com
p. 107 – Figure 52 © Sarah2 / Dreamstime.com
p. 124 – Figure 63 © High Dark Templar,
    http://highdarktemplar.deviantart.com/art/Cat-paw-detail-II-76779823
p. 126 – Tinkerbell © Annaliza Vos
p. 127 – Penny Whistle © Tammy Mustoe
p. 131 – Figure 67 © Designua / Dreamstime.com
p. 133 – Spirit © Shelly Barron
p. 147 – Patch © Robin Clark
p. 149 – Hogan © Cathryn Schreuder
p. 150 – Justice © Pam Brough
p. 151 – Boland © Bernadette de Kock
p. 191 – Diane Budd © Bernadette de Kock

Cover photo © Graham Richardson

All remaining illustrations and photos in this book were created by the author, with support from Tammy Mustoe.

List of Case Studies

CHAPTER 8: Animals in Our Lives

Resources

BOOKS

Bailey, Alice A. *Telepathy and the Etheric Vehicle*. US/UK: Lucis Trust, 2015.

Brennan, Barbara Ann. *Hands of Light*. New York: Bantam Books, 1987.

Ingraham, Caroline. *The Animal Aromatics Workbook: Giving Animals the Choice to Select Their Own Natural Medicines*. UK: Caroline Ingraham, Ltd., 2006.

Ingraham, T.H. *Zoopharmacognosy and Herbal Pharmacology*. UK: T.H. Ingraham, 2011.

Levin, Hilda, Margo Branch, Simon Rappoport, and Derek Mitchell. *A Field Guide to the Mushrooms of South Africa*. Cape Town: Penguin Random House South Africa/Struik Nature, 1995.

Van der Westhuizen, G.C.A. and Albert Eicker. *Field Guide to Mushrooms of Southern Africa*. Cape Town: Penguin Random House South Africa/Struik Nature, 1994.

RECOMMENDED WEBSITES

www.africanis.co.za

https://askabiologist.asu.edu – topic: How animals see color

https://www.cathealth.com – topic: Why cats are stalking things

https://www.lunarplanner.com – topic: Planetary harmonics

Acknowledgments

I could have never managed to write this book without the love and support from those in my life and those who have graced it by passing through. An enormous amount of gratitude and thanks goes to each and every one of my clients and friends who have supported my work throughout the years with their animals. You have embraced and accepted all that I do with open arms and a willingness to hear and learn. We have had many laughs and shed a few tears each step of the way, learning and understanding more about our animals and ourselves. May our journey together continue and grow.

To my nearest and dearest—

To Mom, to whom I could never say thank you enough for all you do: You have stood by my side and supported me through thick and thin in a million different ways. Love you stacks—huge amount of gratitude. Thank you.

To Kyle and Skye, my sons: It has been a privilege and joy to watch you grow and to be by your side every step of the way. I am so proud of the men you are becoming. Thank you for sharing your home with all the never-ending bottles, plants, and smells around the house.

To Milo, Savannah, Romeo, and Molly, my lovely dogs, who have had to sometimes take a backseat when I am away working: You wait patiently for my return and never judge or feel resentful that I have been with other animals and not them. You have been my teachers. You are my heroes.

To Melana Gerber, for sharing this journey as well as your gifts and insights with me: We did it! From the floors of the stables, flying papers, and blunt pencils, a book was born. Melana, I couldn't have done it without you.

To Alexandra, my editor, and mentor: Thank you for always lending an ear and for your optimism and support throughout the years. It means a lot to me.

A huge thank you to all the people behind the scenes who got involved in the book and helped me along the way: Cameron Green and Tammy Mustoe for the illustrations, Bernadette de Kock for some of the photographs, and anyone I may have forgotten.

To everyone who is involved in animal rehabilitation and rescue: Thank you is not said often enough to those of you who devote your free time, effort, and funds so willingly. Thank you for your devotion and tireless commitment to the animals in your care and the rescue work you do.

A special thank you goes to the following people whose animals are featured in the book: Kim – Pony; Jessica – Burning Bright; Inge – Bolla (Boland), Princess, and Ice; Charlene – Brighty; Tammy – Penny Whistle; Annaliza – Tinkerbell; Trudi – Santa; Karena – Tolero; Maryse – Patch; Megan – Gulliver; Estelle – King; Catherine – Hogan; Shelly – Spirit; Pam – Justice; Kim – Taipan; Zay – Hero; Megan – Command and Go; Hailey – Toto; Vicki – Ally; Sue – Tiger; Lucky Lucy Foundation Rescue Center – Mousha; Janna – Abby; Nero – Suzel; and Belinda – Tipi.

About the Author

Photo by Bernadette de Kock

DIANE BUDD is an animal communicator who also practices zoopharma-cognosy, a healing practice in which animals self-select medicinal plant extracts. She is based in Cape Town, South Africa, and has two sons and four dogs. Diane works with all kinds of animals, from rats to horses, and everything in between. She is also the owner of Naturally Green, a company producing natural products for animals.

She has a diploma in Zoopharmacognosy from the Ingraham Academy in the UK and holds certificates in Applied Metaphysics. She both consults and runs regular workshops teaching Animal Communication and Zoopharmacognosy/Self-Selection in Cape Town. You can contact Diane at:

www.healinganimals.co.za
www.naturallygreenpets.co.za,
or diane@healinganimals.co.za;
telephone: 083-383-7533.

FINDHORN PRESS

Life-Changing Books

Learn more about us and our books at
www.findhornpress.com

For information on the Findhorn Foundation:
www.findhorn.org